kids in the kitchen

hamlyn

kids in the kitchen

Sara Lewis

60 FUN AND EASY RECIPES FOR CHILDREN TO MAKE

DEDICATION: To my dear Mum for giving me the freedom to cook when I was young and to my two young children, Alice and William, for sharing their favourite recipes.

First published in Great Britain in 2003
by Hamlyn, a division of Octopus Publishing Ltd
2–4 Heron Quays, London E14 4JP

ISBN 0 600 60745 3

A CIP catalogue record for this book is available from the British Library.

Printed and bound in China

10 9 8 7 6 5 4 3

Notes

Standard level spoon measures are used in all recipes:
1 tablespoon = one 15 ml spoon
1 teaspoon = one 5 ml spoon

Both metric and imperial measurements are given for the recipes. Use one set of measures only, not a mixture of both.

Ovens should be preheated to the specified temperature. If using a fan-assisted oven, follow the manufacturer's instructions for adjusting the time and temperature.

Medium eggs have been used throughout.

A few recipes include nuts and nut derivatives. Anyone with a known nut allergy must avoid these. Children under the age of 3 with a family history of nut allergy, asthma, eczema or any type of allergy are also advised to avoid eating dishes which contain nuts. Do not give whole nuts or seeds to any child under the age of 5 because of risk of choking.

Contents

making food fun

With ready meals now taking up more and more supermarket space, we are in danger of bringing up a generation of children who can't or don't want to cook. OK, so fast food has a place – kids love fish fingers and burgers, but let's keep them as an occasional meal. Encouraging children to cook is fun, you don't need to invest in lots of equipment, and you can eat the end result!

Recipes can be as easy or as complicated as you choose. With the 60 featured in this book, there is something for everyone, from easy ones for tiny cooks to cakes and cookies, main meals and puddings for more adept cooks.

Children find it really rewarding to serve up dishes they've cooked themselves. What child will not blush with pride when met with cries of 'Did you really cook this?' or 'Is there any more?' It can also be a great way to motivate fussy eaters. Mealtimes can become very pressurized if children seem to leave more than they actually eat. Cooking together is relaxing and, as children smell and feel the food they prepare, they may feel more confident and adventurous and more willing to try something new.

As a bonus, cooking together encourages family fun and is educational without being noticeable! Very young children quickly learn new skills in an entertaining way – weighing out ingredients familiarizes them with numbers, while mixing, spreading and spooning aid co-ordination. For older children, cooking on their own brings an added independence and an understanding of how ingredients work together. I can still remember the thrill of the first Sunday lunch I cooked – honey baked ham followed by apple puffs – at the age of 11. My mother hated cooking and was more than happy that my friend, Denise, and I had Saturday afternoon cake-making sessions. We must have made a dreadful mess, but our efforts were always greeted with enthusiasm, and it is an enthusiasm for food that we as a nation are sometimes accused of lacking.

My own children love to cook and have been cooking with me since they could stand on a chair. I still cook with my young son William, aged 9, but my older daughter, Alice, now cooks happily with her friends. I hope that their passion for cooking will stay with them and grow as mine has done. What better gift to give your child than a love of food, made to share with friends and family?

getting started

If you suddenly get the urge to cook, great – seize the moment – but do make sure that you have everything you need before you actually begin to mix. Yes, it sounds very dull and boring, but nothing will make you feel more fed up or cross than getting halfway through a recipe to find that you are missing a vital ingredient.

Weighing and measuring

Careful measuring of ingredients is vital for successful results – this sounds boring, but it's true. The recipes are written in both metric and imperial measurements. Whichever one you choose to follow, stick with the same one all through the recipe, don't mix and match.

Weighing and measuring can also be educational, helping to teach children:

• co-ordination
• the importance of accuracy
• basic number and addition skills
• the idea of volume

…without their really realizing it!

Scales

If you don't have any kitchen scales, or the ones you do have are a bit elderly, encouraging your children to cook may be just the excuse you need for a new set. The modern 'add and weigh' electronic scales are the easiest and most child-friendly to use. Electronic numbers indicate weights with pin-point accuracy and help with number skills. They are available in a wide range of trendy designs and prices. If you are on a tight budget, opt for a mechanical 'add and weigh' set of scales. Traditional balance scales can be trickier for children to use, unless they

Electronic scales are the easiest to use.

have a pointer to show that the correct weight has been reached. They also tend to be much more expensive.

Spoons

Make sure you use measuring teaspoon and tablespoons, and that you level the surface. A well-rounded spoon will contain almost double the amount of a flat one, which will really affect results, especially when you are using baking powder, spices or salt. If you don't have any measuring spoons then they can be bought from large supermarkets, cookware departments in large stores and some hardware shops.

Measuring jugs

For liquids use a plastic jug. Fill to the right amount, then double check by putting the jug on a hard surface and bending down or standing on a chair so that your eye is at the same level as the liquid.

Before you begin

Rummage through the cupboard, refrigerator or freezer and put all the equipment and ingredients on the work surface. (In the recipes the equipment and ingredients are listed in order of use.) Check you have the right tin or dish to cook it in or paper cases or paper to line, then get started.

Basic equipment

Most of the equipment used in this book will be the kind of things that you have at home already. Food processors and electric whisks have been given as an option to help save time and effort, but if you don't have them, there are tips on what to do instead.

Using a microwave

You probably already know this, but for those who are unsure always use china, heavy glass bowls, like pyrex, or plastic ware in the microwave. Avoid metal or plates or cups with silver or gold decoration, which will make sparks when the microwave is turned on. Unglazed pottery tends to get hot, so avoid this too. If you need to cover food, then use microwaveable clingfilm or a plate.

Using a food processor

You can use a food processor for mixing cakes, making pastry and breadcrumbs, finely chopping vegetables, blending soups or fruit until smooth and mixing milk shakes.

Make sure that the blade is firmly secured in the base of the processor and click the lid securely into position. As the motor is very powerful, blend the ingredients for just a minute or two and then have a look. If you need to add any food during blending, add it through the feeder tube at the top and keep the spoon or your fingers well above the top of the tube. Don't attempt to get anything out of the bowl until the blade has stopped turning. Remember that the blade is very sharp, so lift it from the plastic centre and not the metal edges.

Using a liquidizer

Use for making breadcrumbs, blending fruit or soups until smooth and mixing milk shakes.

Smaller than a food processor, this machine must also only be used when the lid is securely fitted. Tiny foods like pieces of bread may be added through the smaller central hole, but only with great care. Never try to stir foods with a spoon when the machine is running. Make sure the machine has stopped completely before you remove the lid and spoon the mixture out with a spoon because the small fixed blades at the base are very sharp.

Using an electric whisk

Use for mixing cakes, whisking egg whites or making pastry.

Some whisks have a stand while others must be hand held while they

SAFETY

Using electric machines saves lots of time and effort, but they must be used with great care. Before you begin, check that:

- the electricity is off
- the machine is well back on the work surface
- there are no trailing electric leads
- that the machine is not near water
- that the blades or beaters are firmly in place

are working. Generally smaller than the other two machines, they will have metal whisk-like blades that must be carefully attached before use. Always check that the electricity is switched off before you do this. As with the other two machines, don't stir ingredients while the blades are running.

all about cooking

Cooking is a bit like learning to read and, as with reading, if you get to know the basic elements first, the rest falls easily into place. The most frequently used techniques are explained and illustrated on the next few pages, so if you're not sure how to prepare fruit and vegetables, grate cheese, rub butter into flour or line a baking tin, read on.

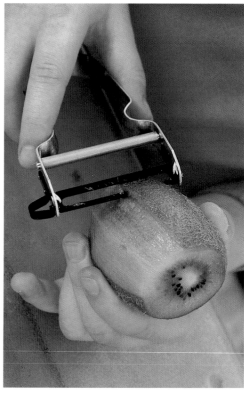

Scrubbing vegetables

- Rinse off the worst of the soil under cold running water.
- Scrub off the stubborn dirt with a small nail brush (kept just for this job).
- Rinse the last traces of dirt and soil under cold running water, then drain well.

Peeling vegetables and fruit

- A swivel-bladed vegetable peeler is the easiest and suits left- or right-handed cooks. Hold the vegetable or fruit firmly in one hand or press against a chopping board.
- Run the peeler along the length of the vegetable or fruit, moving the blade away from you or towards you – whichever feels most comfortable.
- Continue until all the peel has been taken off, then rinse with cold water and drain.

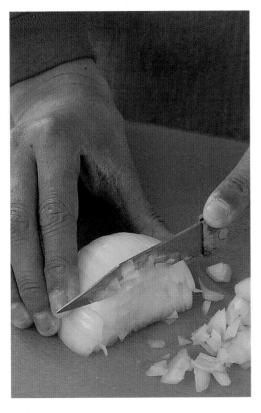  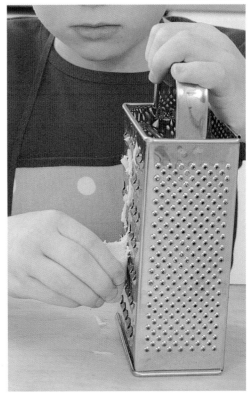

Onions

- Cut the top and hairy root off the onion, but leave a little of the root base on the onion so that it doesn't fall apart.
- Cut in half from the top down to the root end, then peel off the skin.
- Cut each half of the onion into thin slices with a small knife.
- Alternatively, make crossways cuts almost through to the root, then make downward cuts so that the onion is cut into very small pieces.

Peppers

- Stand the pepper on a chopping board so that the green stem is at the top. Cut down through the stem to the bottom of the pepper, cutting it in half.
- Lay the halves down, cut out the white core and green stem with a small knife, then pull away by hand.
- Rinse away the tiny white seeds under cold running water. Cut the flesh into strips or squares, as required.

Root ginger

- Measure and cut a chunk off the root.
- Cut away the brown skin with a small knife or vegetable peeler.
- Grate on a grater or chop finely.

Cutting sticks

- Cut the fruit or vegetables into long thick slices.
- Cut each slice into strips, the same width as the thickness of the slice.
- If you have lots to cut, stack slices on top of each other, then cut into sticks. For just a few slices, you may find it easier to cut one slice at a time into strips. Chefs call these very thin strips 'julienne strips' or just juliennes.

Dicing

- Cut vegetables, meat or Cheddar cheese into thick slices.
- Cut each slice into strips.
- Keeping these strips together, cut across them to make small squares known as dice (think of the small square playing dice).

Getting rid of pips and seeds

- Scoop the seeds and pips from halved melons, papaya or butternut squash with a metal dessertspoon.
- If there are lots of tiny seeds in raspberries or watermelon, puréed fruit can be pressed through a fine sieve with a spoon and the seeds thrown away.

Crushing garlic

- Pull off one clove or piece from the garlic bulb.
- Peel off the papery covering with your fingers.
- Put the garlic into a garlic crusher and press the handle down firmly so that the garlic is squeezed out of the tiny holes.
- Older children may like to chop using a large cook's knife and a chopping board instead of a garlic crusher. Hold the handle of the knife with one hand and the tip of the knife with the other – make sure that your fingers touch only the very top part of the blade – then cut with a seesaw or rocking action until the garlic been chopped into tiny pieces.

Chopping herbs

- Hold the bunch of herbs like a bunch of flowers and use scissors to snip the leaves into a bowl.
- Older children may like to chop using a large cook's knife and a chopping board. Hold the handle of the knife with one hand and the tip of the knife with the other – make sure that your fingers touch only the very top part of the blade – then cut with a seesaw or rocking action until all the leaves have been chopped into tiny pieces.

Squeezing citrus fruit

- Cut the orange, lemon or lime in half on a chopping board, then press each half on to a squeezer. Twist the fruit backwards and forwards, pressing down firmly. Strain the juice into a bowl to remove the pips.

13

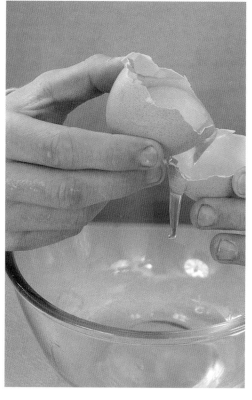

Using a sieve

- Rest the handle and edges of the sieve over a bowl or saucepan.
- Add the ingredient to be sieved, such as icing sugar or flour, then press through the holes of the sieve with a the back of a spoon. For large quantities of puréed fruit, you may find it easier to press using the back of a ladle or a vegetable masher.

Using a pestle and mortar

- Put the spices into the bowl or mortar and grind with the spoon-like pestle. If you don't have a pestle and mortar, improvise with a small bowl or mug and the end of a rolling pin.

Eggs

Cracking an egg

- Holding the egg with both hands, tap the centre of the shell over the rim of a small bowl.
- Carefully enlarge the crack with your fingers until the shell is almost in two halves, then tip the egg into the bowl.

Separating an egg

- Crack the egg, then carefully tip the egg yolk from one half shell to the other so that the yolk stays whole and the white gradually slips into the bowl beneath.
- When the egg white is completely in the bowl, tip the yolk into another bowl and scoop out any tiny pieces of egg yolk within the egg shell.

  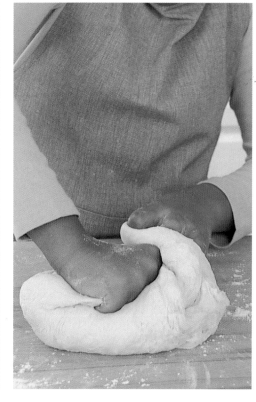

Whisking egg whites

- Whisk egg whites with a balloon or a rotary metal whisk or an electric whisk until they change from a clear liquid to fluffy, thick white mountain peaks.
- When you can see they are really thick, try turning the bowl upside down. They won't slide out if they are ready!

Rubbing in (crumble)

- Cut the butter or margarine into small squares and add to the flour in a bowl.
- Lift a little flour and butter out of the bowl and, with the palms of your hands facing uppermost, rub the flour and fat across your fingers with your thumbs.
- Keep doing this until the pieces of butter or margarine get smaller and smaller and eventually look like fine crumbs.

Kneading bread dough

- Put the bread dough on to a lightly floured work surface, then fold half of the dough back over itself.
- Using the heel or palm of your hand, gently push the dough away from you to stretch the dough.
- Use your other hand to turn the dough slightly and continue with this action over and over again for about 5 minutes until the dough is smooth and elastic, adding a little extra flour to the work surface if necessary.

Grating cheese
- With one hand firmly holding a grater on a chopping board or plate and the other gripping the block of cheese, begin to slide the cheese down the side of the grater.
- Lift the block of cheese up to the top of the grater again and continue this action until all the cheese is shredded into small pieces. Take care that you do not graze your fingers on the grater.

Making Parmesan shavings
- Holding a block of Parmesan cheese on its side, push a swivel-bladed vegetable peeler along the length of the cheese to make wafer thin curls or shavings. Use to sprinkle over the top of your favourite pasta dish.

Flaking fish
- Drain canned tuna or salmon or put just-cooked fish fillets on to a plate. Break into pieces with a knife and fork, checking carefully and removing any bones.

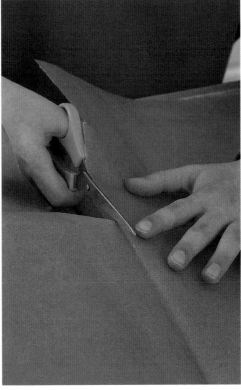

Making breadcrumbs

- Cut the crusts off the bread with a knife and tear the bread into pieces.
- Put the bread into a food processor fitted with a metal blade or use a liquidizer. Insert on to the machine base and check that the lid is secure. Blend until fine crumbs are formed.

Baking tins

Lining the base of a deep tin

- Put the tin on a sheet of greaseproof paper and draw around the outside of the tin with a pencil.
- Cut out the shape and put into the bottom of the tin. Brush the paper and sides of the tin with a little oil.

Lining the base and sides of a deep tin

- Fold a sheet of greaseproof paper into two so that the paper is a little higher than the side of the tin. Make a 1 cm (½ inch) fold up from the long cut edges of the paper.
- Make small cuts up to the fold.
- Stand the paper in the tin with the cuts downward, then add a piece of paper the same size as the base, as before. Brush the paper with a little oil. (If you are using nonstick baking paper, you don't need to brush this with oil.)

Lining a shallow rectangular tin

- Cut a rectangle, a little larger than the tin.
- Lay the paper over the tin and make diagonal cuts into the corners.
- Ease the paper into the tin and tuck the cut corners over one another so that the paper fits snugly. Brush with oil if using greaseproof paper, but nonstick baking paper can be left without oil.

Removing a cake or pudding from a loose-bottomed tin

- Loosen the edges of the cake with a small knife.
- Stand the tin on a can, then gently press down on the tin sides, leaving the cake and the base part of the tin sitting on top of the can, with the side of the tin on the work surface. Use ovengloves if the tin is hot.

When is food cooked?

Pasta

- Lift one strand or piece of pasta out of the saucepan of boiling water with a fork. Cool for a minute or two, or rinse under cold water to cool quickly.
- Bite into the pasta – it should taste tender but still be firm to the touch or bite.

Fish

- Break one of the fish fillets with a knife. If the flesh looks the same colour all the way through, it is ready. If it is two colours, cook for 5 minutes more and check again.

Chicken

- For smaller joints of chicken, cut one of them in half to make sure that it is cooked. If the flesh is slightly pink, cook for about 5 minutes longer and check again.
- For a whole chicken, insert a small knife into the thickest part of the leg and through to the body.
- Wait for a minute or two, then look at the juices that run out. If they are pink, the chicken must go back in the oven for about 15 minutes. If the juices are clear, the chicken is ready.

cook's terms

Bake
to cook food in the oven.

Beat
to soften and mix an ingredient; this is usually done with a wooden spoon.

Blend
to mix; usually the foods that are blended are mixed until they become smooth.

Chop
to cut food into tiny pieces.

Chunks
pieces of food, much larger than diced food.

Colander
metal bowl-like container with handles and holes; used for draining foods like pasta, peas and potatoes.

Cream
to beat butter and sugar or margarine and sugar with a wooden spoon or an electric whisk until a smooth, pale, cream-like mixture; usually used when making cakes.

Dice
to cut foods into small squares.

Drain
to pour off the water from foods that have been soaked or cooked, either with a sieve or colander.

Drizzle
to sprinkle drops of oil over the surface of a dish.

Garnish
to finish a recipe with a savoury decoration, perhaps a sprig of watercress, some herb leaves, a few chopped nuts or a sprinkling of paprika.

Grease
to brush baking tins with a special cook's brush dipped in a little oil so that cakes, biscuits or pastries don't stick during baking.

Grill
to cook foods under the grill.

Fry
to cook foods in a frying pan on the hob with a little oil or butter.

Line
to put greaseproof or nonstick baking paper into the base or the base and the sides of a cake tin, so that the cake or dessert does not stick to it.

Purée
to squash fruit or vegetables in a liquidizer, food processor or by pressing through a sieve to make a smooth, sauce-like mixture.

Sift
to press dry foods such as flour or icing sugar through a sieve to remove the lumps.

Simmer
to cook a liquid in a saucepan so that bubbles just break the surface.

Whisk
to beat air into egg whites or cream using a balloon whisk or electric whisk so that they become thick; alternatively, to beat out any lumps when making a sauce.

safety & hygiene

No matter what your age, here are a few basic reminders on how to avoid a trip to a hospital casualty department and on how to leave the kitchen as you found it. Always check with an adult before you begin cooking to make sure that it is OK.

Safety

- Handle knives and electrical equipment with care and respect.
- Enjoy what you cook but don't play about or you will forget to add a vital ingredient or take something out of the oven too early or, worse still, burn or cut yourself.
- Hot food can burn so stir large pans carefully and keep your hands away from steaming kettles or boiling water.
- Make sure the pan you are using is big enough or the contents will bubble over the top.
- Turn pan handles to the side of the cooker so that they won't get knocked off.
- Always wear ovengloves to take tins or dishes out of the oven.
- Although most dishes do not get hot in a microwave, unglazed pottery does, and food definitely does, so handle with care.
- Mop up any spills.
- Throw away food that has been dropped on the floor so that you don't slip over.
- Turn on the oven before you start, as it takes about 15 minutes to heat up – but don't switch on the hob until you begin cooking as it heats up immediately.
- Remember to turn off the oven when you have finished.

Handle electrical equipment with respect.

Always turn handles to the side of the cooker.

Take care when using a knife.

Hygiene hints

- Always wash your hands before you begin.
- Tie back long hair.
- Only use food that is within its date stamp.
- Wash knives and chopping boards between using raw and cooked meats, or use separate chopping boards.
- Always check that food is cooked right through to the centre.
- Only reheat cooked food once and make sure it is piping hot all the way through.

Look after the kitchen

- Chop or cut foods on a chopping board, not the work surface.
- Put foods straight from the oven on to a heatproof mat so that you don't scorch the work surface.
- Wipe down the work surfaces, wash up the dishes and sweep up the bits on the floor when you've finished cooking.

Don't forget the clearing up!

Cooking is great fun, washing up and tidying up afterwards aren't! Most parents are happy for you to cook unaided, providing it doesn't take them 3 hours to clear up the mess afterwards. Even tiny children can be encouraged to have a go at washing up. Stand them on a sturdy chair and keep the mop handy for the splashes.

Ask for help with difficult tasks.

For very young children

- Stand your child on a sturdy chair so that he or she can reach the work surface. Alternatively, cover the floor with a plastic or PVC tablecloth, then measure and mix while the child sits on the cloth.
- Some little children hate the feel of PVC aprons, so if you don't have a cotton one small enough, use an older brother or sister's outgrown T-shirt as a cover-up.
- Supervise your child closely and help at all stages.
- Allow plenty of time – kids hate to be hurried.

French toast

(1)

equipment

shallow bowl

fork

chopping board

small serrated knife

frying pan

fish slice

ingredients

1 egg

1 tablespoon milk

2 slices fruit bread

15 g (¹/₂ oz) butter

1 tablespoon sunflower oil

1 tablespoon caster sugar

pinch of ground
cinnamon, if liked

few peeled satsuma or
orange segments,
to serve

what to do

(1) • Break the egg into the shallow bowl, add
the milk and beat with a fork until mixed.

2 • Put the fruit bread on the chopping board
and cut the slices into strips or triangles
with the knife.

3 • Heat the butter and oil in the frying pan.

(4) • At the same time, dip a few pieces of
bread into the egg mixture, turning until
they are covered.

• Lift out of the egg mixture, letting the
extra mixture drain back into the bowl.

5 • Add the bread to the frying pan and cook
for 2–3 minutes, turning once with the
fish slice until golden – get adult help
for this.

(4)

6 • Dip and cook the rest of the bread in the same way.

7 • Sprinkle with the sugar and add the cinnamon, if using. Serve with satsuma or orange segments.

tips

★ Cut shapes from plain white sliced bread with biscuit cutters.

★ For a savoury version, use wholemeal bread, omit the sugar and serve with ketchup.

stripy cheese on toast

Serves
1 adult and
1 child

equipment

grill rack
knife
chopping board
small serrated knife

ingredients

2 slices bread

little butter,
for spreading

75 g (3 oz) Cheddar
cheese

75 g (3 oz) red Leicester
cheese

halved cherry tomatoes
and cubes of cucumber,
to serve

what to do

1 • Preheat the grill for 2–3 minutes. Toast the bread under the grill until both sides are lightly browned – get adult help with this.

• Lightly butter the toast.

2 • On the chopping board, cut the cheese into thin fingers, about 5mm (¼ inch) thick and 1.5 cm (¾ inch) wide.

• Cover the bread with different lines of yellow and red cheese until the toast is covered.

3 • Put the toast back under the grill and cook until the cheese is bubbling. Serve with halved cherry tomatoes and cubes of cucumber.

dinner jackets

Serves
2 adults and
2 children

ingredients

4 baking potatoes,
   each weighing about
   200 g (7 oz)

200 g (7 oz) can tuna,
   in water or oil

¹/₂ red pepper

1 small dessert apple

75 g (3 oz) sweetcorn,
   defrosted if frozen

3 tablespoons mayonnaise

3 tablespoons natural
   yogurt

salt and pepper

equipment

nail brush

fork

piece of kitchen paper

can opener

small bowl

chopping board

small knife

spoon

tea towel or ovengloves

what to do

① • Set the oven to 200°C/400°F/Gas Mark 6.

• Scrub the potatoes and prick them with
  a fork.

• Bake in the oven for 1¼ hours until soft.
  Alternatively, cook in the microwave on
  a piece of kitchen paper for about
  10 minutes on Full Power, or according to
  manufacturer's instructions, until soft.

2 • Meanwhile, to make the filling, first open
  the can of tuna and drain off the liquid.

• Tip the tuna into the bowl and break it
  into pieces with the fork.

③ • On the chopping board, cut the red
  pepper in half, cut away the white core
  and scrape away the seeds.

• Cut the red pepper into tiny squares.

4 • Cut the apple into four pieces, remove the core and cut into tiny squares.

• Add the red pepper and apple to the tuna with the sweetcorn, mayonnaise, yogurt and a little salt and pepper. Mix together with the spoon.

5 • Hold the cooked potato in a clean tea towel or ovengloves and cut it in half or cut a cross in the top – get adult help with this. Cut the other potatoes in the same way.

• Put the potatoes on to plates and spoon the tuna mixture over the top. Serve at once.

popcorn

ingredients

2 tablespoons
sunflower oil

100 g (3½ oz) popping
corn

50 g (2 oz) butter

6 tablespoons maple
syrup

Serves 4
children

equipment

large heavy based
saucepan with lid

wooden spoon

coloured paper cups
or cones, to serve

what to do

1 • Put the oil in the saucepan, add the
popcorn in a single layer and put the lid
on the saucepan.

• Begin to cook over a medium heat – get
adult help with this. As the popcorn warms
up you will hear loud bangs and pops as
the popcorn hits the side of the pan.

2 • Shake the pan from time to time to
encourage the last few popcorn kernels to
cook – get adult help for this.

• When the pan is quiet, turn off the heat,
lift the lid and carefully look inside the
pan. It should be full of white puffy
popcorn. If there are still lots of popcorn
kernels, put the lid back on and cook for a
little longer.

3 • Add the butter and maple syrup to the
popcorn and toss together using the
wooden spoon – remember that the
saucepan will be hot.

• Spoon the popcorn into coloured paper
cups or cones of paper to serve.

tip
★ Why not try tossing the popcorn with some puréed strawberries, jam or butter and honey?

mini vegetable frittatas

Makes 12

equipment

nail brush or vegetable peeler

chopping board

small knife

small saucepan

colander

pastry brush

12-hole nonstick muffin or bun tin

grater

large jug

ovengloves

ingredients

250 g (8 oz) baking potatoes

125 g (4 oz) frozen mixed vegetables

little oil, for brushing

75 g (3 oz) Cheddar, Gruyère or Emmental cheese

6 eggs

150 ml ($\frac{1}{4}$ pint) milk

salt and pepper

vegetable sticks and tomato ketchup, to serve

what to do

(1) • Set the oven to 190°C/375°F/Gas Mark 5.

• Scrub or peel the potatoes, place them on the chopping board and cut into small squares.

• Put the potatoes into the saucepan with the frozen vegetables, cover with cold water then bring to the boil.

• Cook for 4 minutes until the potatoes are just tender. Drain them into a colander – get adult help for this.

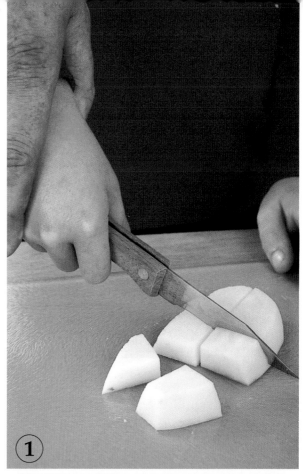

(1)

(3)

2 • Use a pastry brush to brush the holes in the muffin or bun tin with a little oil.

• Grate the cheese on the grater, then divide the cheese and vegetables among the holes in the tray.

3 • Beat the eggs, milk and a little salt and pepper together in the large jug. Pour equally over the potatoes and vegetables.

• Put the tin in the centre of the oven and cook for 10 minutes until the tops are golden and the eggs are set – get adult help with this. Serve warm or cold with veggy sticks (see page 12) and ketchup.

31

baby apple muffins

(2)

Makes 12

ingredients

1 Gala dessert apple

50 g (2 oz) soft margarine

50 g (2 oz) caster sugar

50 g (2 oz) self-raising flour

1 egg

4 tablespoons cream cheese

few candy-coated chocolate drops, sugar flowers or sugar sprinkles, to decorate

equipment

12-hole petit four tray

12 mini paper cases

grater

mixing bowl

wooden spoon or electric mixer

ovengloves

what to do

1 • Set the oven to 180°C/350°F/Gas Mark 4. Line the 12–hole petit four tray with the little paper cases.

(2) • Coarsely grate the apple, still with the peel on, and discard the core – get adult help with this.

(3) • Put the soft margarine into the mixing bowl and add the sugar, flour and egg. Beat with the wooden spoon or electric mixer until smooth.

(2)

(3)

4 • Stir in the apple, then spoon the muffin mixture into the paper cases.

• Bake in the centre of the oven for 10 minutes until well risen and golden and the tops of the muffins spring back when pressed with fingertips. Leave to cool in the tin.

5 • Spread the top of each cooled muffin with a little cream cheese, then decorate with chocolate drops, sugar flowers or sugar sprinkles.

marshmallow crunchies

Makes 30

equipment

large saucepan

wooden spoon or plastic spatula

heatproof mat

pastry brush

small roasting tin, about 18 x 28 cm (7 x 11 inches)

small serrated knife

paper cake cases

ingredients

75 g (3 oz) butter

3 tablespoons golden syrup

200 g (7 oz) pack pink and white marshmallows

125 g (4 oz) toasted rice breakfast cereal

oil, for brushing

50 g (2 oz) coloured mini marshmallows

what to do

1 • Put the butter, golden syrup and marshmallows into the saucepan and heat gently, stirring with the wooden spoon, until melted – get adult help with this.

2 • Take the pan off the heat and put on the heatproof mat. Stir in the cereal and mix well.

3 • Brush the sides and base of the roasting tin with a little oil, add the marshmallow mixture and press flat with the wooden spoon or plastic spatula.

• Chill in the refrigerator until set.

4 • Cut into squares with the knife, lift out of the tin, arrange in paper cases, decorate with mini marshmallows and serve.

tips

★ The butter, syrup and marshmallows can be warmed in the microwave for 1–1½ minutes on Full Power or according to the manufacturer's instructions. Remember to use a bowl without any metal bits and to remove it from the microwave with a tea towel or ovengloves as the bowl may get hot.

★ The marshmallow mixture can be spooned straight into paper cases if preferred.

no bake chocolate cake

Makes 16 pieces

equipment

medium saucepan

wooden spoon

kitchen scissors

plastic bag

rolling pin

loose-bottomed fluted flan tin, 23 cm (9 inches)

small sieve

ingredients

300 g (10 oz) luxury plain cooking chocolate

75 g (3 oz) butter

2 tablespoons golden syrup

405 g (13 oz) can sweetened condensed milk

175 g (6 oz) exotic ready-to-eat dried fruits

125 g (4 oz) sultanas

200 g (7 oz) rich tea biscuits

little cocoa powder (optional)

what to do

1 • Break the chocolate into the saucepan, add the butter, syrup and condensed milk.

• Heat gently, stirring from time to time with the wooden spoon, until the chocolate has melted – get adult help with this.

2 • Cut the exotic fruit into pieces with the scissors, then stir into the melted chocolate with the sultanas.

3 • Put the biscuits into the plastic bag and seal the top of the bag.

②

③

tip

★ Older children may like to add 150 g (5 oz) roughly chopped hazelnuts or almonds, or a mixture of them both. Do not give whole or roughly chopped nuts to children under 5 years old.

• Crush the biscuits with a rolling pin until they are broken into chunky pieces. Stir them into the chocolate mixture.

4 • Tip the mixture into the loose-bottomed flan tin and press into an even layer.

• Chill the cake in the refrigerator for at least 4 hours until it is firm.

5 • Stand the flan tin on a can, then press the tin sides down and away from the base.

• Dust the top with a little sifted cocoa, if using, then cut into thin slices to serve. Store in the refrigerator.

pink blush strawberry smoothie

equipment

small knife

chopping board

liquidizer or food processor

ingredients

4 strawberries

1 small ripe banana

1 ripe peach or nectarine

150 g (5 oz) pot strawberry yogurt

1 teaspoon honey

150 ml (¹/₄ pint) apple or orange juice

what to do

1 • Remove the green tops of the strawberries, then cut the strawberries in half with the knife on the chopping board.

• Peel and thickly slice the banana.

• Cut the peach or nectarine in half, take out the stone and slice thickly.

2 • Put all the fruits into the liquidizer or food processor.

• Add the yogurt, honey and fruit juice,

3 • Put the lid carefully on the machine and blend together – get adult help with this. Pour into one or two glasses and serve.

38

tip

★ Try making a smoothie with 1 small mango and the juice of 1 lime instead of the peach and strawberries, or experiment and make up your own flavour combinations.

carrot and tomato soup

Serves
2 adults and
2 children

equipment

chopping board

small knife

vegetable peeler

medium saucepan
with lid

wooden spoon

ingredients

1 onion

1 large carrot

1 medium potato

500 g (1 lb) tomatoes

1–2 garlic cloves

1 tablespoon olive oil

900 ml (1½ pints)
vegetable or chicken
stock

3 teaspoons sun-dried
or ordinary tomato
paste

2 teaspoons caster sugar

salt and pepper

small bunch fresh basil,
to serve (optional)

what to do

①
- On the chopping board, peel and finely chop the onion.

- Peel and cut the carrot and potato into small cubes.

- Wash and chop the tomatoes.

- Peel and crush the garlic (see page 13).

2
- Heat the oil in the saucepan, add the onion and fry over a medium heat for 5 minutes, stirring from time to time with the wooden spoon, until pale golden.

3 • Stir in the carrot, potato, tomatoes and garlic, then add the stock, tomato paste, sugar and a little salt and pepper.

• Bring the mixture to the boil, cover and simmer for 20 minutes.

4 • Tear the basil leaves into pieces and stir half into the soup. Ladle into bowls and sprinkle the rest of the basil over the top. Serve with warm crusty bread.

tip

★ If you prefer smooth soups, blend the finished soup in a liquidizer or food processor. Reheat to serve if necessary.

cashew dip and veggie dunkers

Serves
2 adults and
2 children

equipment

grill pan

foil

liquidizer, food processor
or spice mill

chopping board

small knife

small bowl and large
plate, to serve

vegetable peeler

spoon

ingredients

100 g (3¹/₂ oz) cashew
nuts

200 ml (7 fl oz) Greek
or thick natural yogurt

1 spring onion

salt and pepper

2 teaspoons olive oil

little paprika

2 carrots

¹/₄ cucumber

few breadsticks,
for dipping (optional)

what to do

1 • Line the grill pan with foil. Put the nuts
on the foil and cook until lightly browned.

• Tip them into the liquidizer, food
processor or spice mill and grind to make
a fine powder.

2 • Mix the nuts into the yogurt.

• On the chopping board, trim each end of
the spring onion, then thinly slice. Stir
into the nut mixture and add salt and
pepper to taste.

• Spoon the dip into the small bowl, set on
the large plate.

- Drizzle the dip with the olive oil and sprinkle with paprika.

(3) • Peel the carrots with the vegetable peeler, then cut into sticks.

- Wash the cucumber and cut it into sticks.

- Arrange the veggie sticks and breadsticks around the dip and serve.

tip

★ Do not give whole nuts to children under 5 years old.

carrot and rosemary risotto

Serves
2 adults and
2 children

equipment

chopping board

small knife

vegetable peeler

kitchen scissors

frying pan

wooden spoon

large jug

ladle

grater

ingredients

1 onion

250 g (8 oz) carrots

1–2 garlic cloves

few stems fresh
rosemary

2 tablespoons olive oil

250 g (8 oz) risotto
(arborio) rice

1 litre (1³/₄ pints)
chicken, lamb or
vegetable stock

what to do

(1) • On the chopping board peel and finely
chop the onion.

• Peel the carrots with the vegetable peeler
and cut into small squares.

• Peel and crush the garlic (see page 13).

• Snip the rosemary into small pieces using
the scissors.

2 • Heat the oil in the frying pan, add the
onion and fry for 5 minutes over
medium heat, stirring from time to time
with the wooden spoon until the onion is
pale golden.

3 • Stir in the carrots, garlic, 1 tablespoon of the rosemary leaves and the rice.

• Heat the stock and add it to the jug. Pour one quarter of the hot stock on to the rice and simmer.

• Keep a watch on the risotto as it cooks and top up with ladlefuls of stock every 5 minutes or so until the rice is soft and the stock nearly all added. This should take about 20 minutes.

4 • Spoon the risotto into warmed shallow dishes and top with the extra rosemary leaves, if liked.

tip

★ Alternatively, serve with a little grated Parmesan cheese on top of the risotto.

monster munch salad

(2)

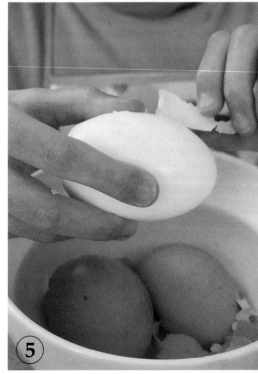

(5)

Serves
1 adult and
2 children

equipment

small saucepan

lemon squeezer

kitchen scissors

small bowl

colander

large salad bowl

chopping board

vegetable peeler

grater

small knife

can opener

fork

ingredients

3 eggs

1/2 lemon

few stems fresh
 tarragon (optional)

3 tablespoons
 mayonnaise

1 teaspoon honey or
 maple syrup

salt and pepper

1 cos lettuce

1 carrot

1/4 cucumber

200 g (7 oz) can tuna
 or salmon in water
 or oil

200 g (7 oz) can
 cannellini or red
 kidney beans

what to do

1 • Put the eggs into the small saucepan,
 cover with cold water and bring to the
 boil. Simmer for 8 minutes until
 hardboiled.

(2) • Meanwhile, squeeze the lemon and snip
 the tarragon with the scissors, if using.

 • Mix the lemon juice, 1 tablespoon
 tarragon, the mayonnaise and honey or
 syrup in the small bowl with a little salt
 and pepper.

3 • Separate the lettuce leaves, throwing away
 the coarse outer leaves. Wash with cold
 water and drain in a colander. Tear into
 pieces and put into the large salad bowl.

- Drizzle the dressing over and toss together.

4
- On the chopping board, peel the carrot with the vegetable peeler, then grate into the dish.
- Dice the cucumber.
- Open the can of tuna or salmon, and drain and break the fish into pieces with the fork.
- Open and drain the beans.

- Add all these ingredients to the salad bowl and mix gently.

(5)
- Drain the hardboiled eggs, rinse with cold water to cool quickly, crack the shells and peel the eggs.
- Cut the eggs into thick slices and arrange on top of the salad.

toad in the hole

ingredients

125 g (4 oz) plain flour

salt and pepper

small bunch fresh thyme

1 egg

300 ml (½ pint) milk and water mixed

500 g (1 lb) extra lean pork sausages

8 rashers streaky bacon

2 tablespoons sunflower oil

Serves 2 adults and 2 children

equipment

large bowl

balloon whisk

chopping board

kitchen scissors

small knife

small roasting tin

ovengloves

what to do

(1) • Set the oven to 220°C/425°F/Gas Mark 7.

• Put the flour and salt and pepper into the bowl.

• Tear the leaves off the thyme stems and add 2 tablespoons to the bowl along with the egg.

• Gradually whisk in the milk and water until the batter is smooth and frothy.

(2) • On the chopping board, separate the sausages with the scissors or small knife.

• Stretch each rasher of bacon by running the flat of the knife along the rasher until it is half as long again.

• Wrap the bacon around the sausages.

1

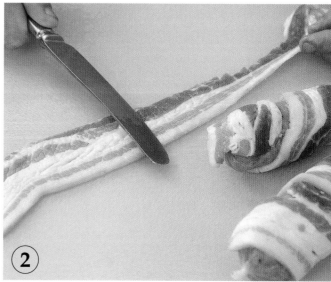

2

3 • Pour the oil into the roasting tin and add the bacon-wrapped sausages. Cook in the oven for 5 minutes until sizzling. Whisk the batter again.

4 • Take the tin out of the oven with the ovengloves and quickly pour in the batter – get adult help with this.

• Put the tin back into the oven and cook for about 20 minutes until the batter is well risen and golden. Serve hot with baked beans.

oriental chicken

Serves
2 adults and
2 children

ingredients

2 tablespoons hoisin sauce

2 tablespoons soy sauce

2 tablespoons sunflower oil

4 boneless, skinless chicken breasts, about 625 g (1¼ lb) in total

200 g (7 oz) broccoli

200 g (7 oz) long-grain white rice

125 g (4 oz) frozen peas

thin strips red pepper or carrot, to garnish (optional)

equipment

shallow china or glass dish

tablespoon

chopping board

small knife

medium saucepan

grill rack

sheet of foil

fork

sieve

what to do

① • Mix together the hoisin sauce, soy sauce and oil in the base of the shallow china or glass dish.

• Rinse the chicken with cold water, drain well and add to dish.

• Spoon over the hoisin mixture, then turn over the chicken and spread the mixture over the second side. Set aside for 15 minutes.

② • On the chopping board, cut the broccoli into tiny florets and the stems into slices.

• Half-fill the saucepan with cold water, bring to the boil and add the rice. Cook for 6 minutes.

• Add the broccoli and peas and cook for 4 minutes.

①

②

3 • Meanwhile, preheat the grill for 2–3 minutes.

• Line the grill rack with foil, add the chicken breasts and grill for 10 minutes, turning once or twice until evenly browned – get adult help with this.

• Transfer the chicken to the chopping board, steady the chicken with the fork and cut into thick slices. There should be no pink juices, if there are, quickly put chicken back under the grill for 3–4 minutes.

4 • Drain the rice into the sieve, spoon on to serving plates and top with the chicken slices. Garnish with thin slices of red pepper or carrot, if liked.

cous cous with grilled sausages

ingredients

500 g (1 lb) extra lean pork sausages

125 g (4 oz) cous cous

25 g (1 oz) sultanas

200 ml (7 fl oz) boiling water

50 g (2 oz) green beans

50 g (2 oz) frozen peas

2 tomatoes

½ orange

1 garlic clove

2 tablespoons olive oil

salt and pepper

Serves
2 adults and
2 children

equipment

grill rack

fork or tongs

large bowl

measuring jug

chopping board

small knife

small saucepan

colander

lemon squeezer

what to do

(1) • Preheat the grill for 1–2 minutes.

• Put the sausages on the grill rack and cook under the grill for 10 minutes, turning once or twice with the fork or tongs – get adult help with this.

(2) • Meanwhile, put the cous cous and sultanas into the bowl.

• Pour over the boiling water and leave to soak for 5 minutes.

3 • On the chopping board, cut the green beans into thick slices.

• Put the beans into the small saucepan with the peas. Cover with cold water, bring to the boil and cook for 4 minutes.

4 • Drain the beans and peas in the colander – get adult help with this.

• Chop the tomatoes. Squeeze the juice from the orange using the lemon squeezer. Crush the garlic (see page 13).

5 • Stir the vegetables, juice, garlic, oil and a little salt and pepper into the cous cous and mix together well. Spoon on to plates and top with the sausages.

53

Serves
2 adults and
2 children

equipment

chopping board

small knife

vegetable peeler

medium saucepan
with lid

wooden spoon

can opener

small saucepan

sieve

grater

shallow heatproof dish

spicy tortillas

ingredients

1 onion

2 carrots

2 garlic cloves

1 tablespoon olive oil

500 g (1 lb) extra lean
minced beef

2 teaspoons mild paprika

1 teaspoon ground cumin

415 g (13½ oz) can
baked beans

400 g (13 oz) can
chopped tomatoes

200 ml (7 fl oz) chicken
or beef stock

salt and pepper

Topping

125 g (4 oz) mixed
frozen vegetables

125 g (4 oz) original
tortilla chips

75 g (3 oz) Cheddar or
mozzarella cheese

what to do

1 • On the chopping board, peel and chop
the onion.

• Peel the carrots with the vegetable peeler
and cut into small squares.

• Peel and crush the garlic (see page 13).

② • Heat the oil in the saucepan and add the
mince, onion, carrots and garlic. Fry,
stirring with the wooden spoon, until the
mince is evenly browned.

3 • Stir in the paprika and cumin and cook for
1 minute. Add the baked beans, tomatoes,
stock and salt and pepper.

②

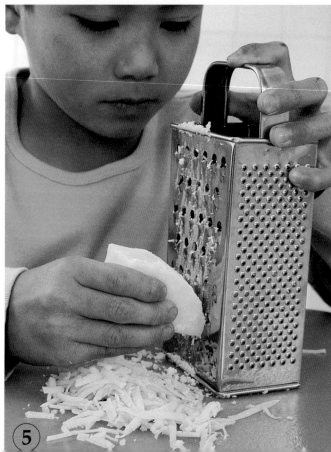

⑤

- Bring to the boil, breaking up any large pieces of mince with the spoon. Cover and cook gently for 45 minutes, stirring from time to time so that it doesn't stick.

4 • When the mince is cooked, put the frozen vegetables into the small saucepan, cover with cold water, bring to the boil and cook for 4 minutes. Drain into the sieve.

(5) • Spoon the mince mixture into the shallow heatproof dish. Sprinkle the vegetables over and top with the tortilla chips.

- Preheat the grill for 2–3 minutes. Grate the cheese and sprinkle over the dish. Cook under the grill until the cheese is bubbling, then spoon on to plates.

baked salmon parcels

Serves
2 adults and
2 children

equipment

colander
4 sheets of foil
chopping board
vegetable peeler
small knife
grater
lemon squeezer
baking sheet
medium saucepan
kitchen scissors
sieve
ovengloves

ingredients

4 salmon fillets, about
  625 g (1¼ lb) in total

salt and pepper

2 carrots

4 spring onions

1 small red pepper

2.5 cm (1 inch) piece
  root ginger

2 limes

150 g (5 oz) reduced fat
  coconut milk

200 g (7 oz) basmati or
  jasmine rice

bunch fresh coriander

what to do

① • Set the oven to 180°C/350°F/Gas Mark 4.

 • Put the salmon in the colander and rinse
with cold water. Drain and put each piece
on a separate piece of foil, with the skin
downwards. Add salt and pepper and fold
up the edges of the foil.

② • On the chopping board, peel and cut the
carrot into thin strips.

 • Trim each end of the spring onions and
cut into thin strips.

 • Cut the core and seeds away from red
pepper and cut into thin strips. Peel and
grate the ginger.

3 • Cut one of the limes in half and squeeze the juice using the lemon squeezer. Sprinkle this over the salmon.

• Divide the vegetables and ginger among the parcels. Spoon 3 tablespoons coconut milk and 1 tablespoon water around each piece of salmon. Fold up edges of the foil to make a parcel, then put these on to the baking sheet.

4 • Cook in the centre of the oven for 10 minutes.

• Meanwhile, half-fill the saucepan with cold water and bring to the boil. Add the rice and simmer for 8–10 minutes until tender.

5 • Reserve some sprigs of coriander and snip the rest with the scissors to give about 6 tablespoons.

• Drain the rice into the sieve, then tip back into the dry pan – get adult help with this.

• Squeeze the juice from the second lime, add to the rice with the snipped coriander, salt and pepper. Toss together, then spoon on to serving plates.

6 • Carefully open the foil parcels and top the rice with the salmon, vegetables and coconut juices. Garnish with sprigs of coriander.

one pan chicken

Serves 2 adults and 2 children

equipment

colander

chopping board

small knife

large roasting tin

ovengloves

ingredients

4 chicken thighs and 4 chicken drumsticks

1 kg (2 lb) baby new potatoes

1 small butternut squash

1 red pepper

1 whole garlic bulb

4 tablespoons olive oil

few stems fresh sage or a little dried sage

salt and pepper

1 teaspoon ground Cajun spice

4 teaspoons runny honey

what to do

① • Set the oven to 200°C/400°F/Gas Mark 6.

• Put the chicken in the colander, rinse with cold water and drain well. On the chopping board, make two or three cuts in each piece of chicken, then put them in the roasting tin.

② • Wash the potatoes and cut any large ones in half on the washed chopping board.

• Cut the butternut squash in half lengthways, scoop out the seeds with the spoon and cut the peel away with the vegetable peeler. Cut into thick slices.

• Cut the red pepper into chunky pieces, discarding the core and seeds. Separate the garlic bulb into cloves but leave their papery skins on.

①

②

③ • Put all the vegetables into the roasting tin.

• Spoon over the oil and add the garlic cloves. Sprinkle with a few sage leaves, salt and pepper and Cajun spice.

4 • Roast in the centre of the oven for 45 minutes. Carefully take the pan out of the oven with ovengloves. Turn the chicken, spoon the oil over the potatoes and drizzle with the honey – get adult help with this. Cook for 15 more minutes until the chicken is thoroughly cooked.

mixed fish skewers

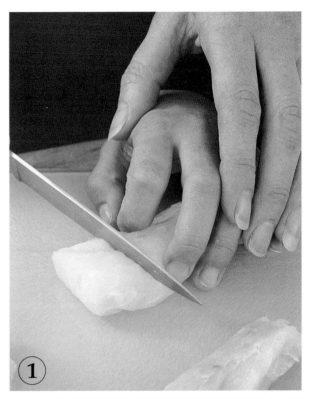

Serves
2 adults and
2 children

ingredients

300 g (10 oz) salmon
  fillet, skinned

300 g (10 oz) haddock
  fillet, skinned

½ lemon

3 teaspoons Dijon
  mustard

2 teaspoons muscovado
  sugar

3 tablespoons olive oil

salt and pepper

200 g (7 oz) crème
  fraîche

few stems fresh dill

few cos lettuce leaves

lemon wedges, to serve
  (optional)

equipment

chopping board

small knife

8 small metal or
  wooden skewers

foil

grill rack

lemon squeezer

2 small bowls

kitchen scissors

colander

what to do

(1) • Rinse both types of fish with cold water.
    Drain well, then place on the chopping
    board and cut into cubes about 2 cm
    (¾ inch) big.

  • Thread alternate colours of fish on to eight
    small skewers. Line the grill rack with foil
    and add the skewers.

2 • Squeeze the juice from the lemon and mix
    with 2 teaspoons of the mustard, the
    sugar, oil and a little salt and pepper in
    the small bowl. Spoon half over the fish.

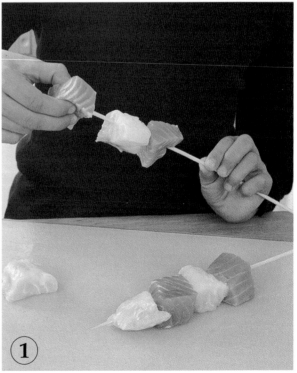

3 • Preheat the grill for 2–3 minutes, then cook the fish for 3 minutes.

• Carefully, turn the skewers over and spoon over the rest of the oil mixture. Grill for 3 more minutes until the fish breaks easily when pressed with a knife.

tip
★ Make sure you use fish that is already skinned to save a messy job.

4 • Meanwhile, mix the rest of the mustard with the crème fraîche.

• Snip the dill into pieces with the scissors and add 2 teaspoons along with some salt and pepper. Spoon into the other small bowl.

• Rinse the lettuce with cold water, drain in a colander and arrange on serving plates. Top with skewer and serve with lemon wedges, if liked, and spoonfuls of sauce.

sticky barbecued ribs

Serves
2 adults and
2 children

equipment

colander

large roasting tin

small bowl

pastry brush

measuring jug

chopping board

small knife

ovengloves

ingredients

1.25 kg (2¹/₂ lb) pork ribs

5 tablespoons tomato ketchup

3 tablespoons soft light brown sugar

2 tablespoons sunflower oil

2 tablespoons Worcestershire sauce

2 teaspoons Dijon mustard

450 ml (³/₄ pint) chicken stock

2 oranges, cut in wedges, to serve

what to do

1 • Set the oven to 200°C/400°F/Gas Mark 6.

• Put the ribs into a colander, rinse with cold water, drain well and put into the roasting tin.

② • Mix the ketchup, sugar, oil, Worcestershire sauce and mustard together in a small bowl. Brush the mixture over the ribs with the pastry brush.

• Measure the stock in the jug and pour it into the base of the tin.

3 • Roast in the centre of the oven for 1¼ hours, brushing once or twice with pan juices and turning the very brown ribs over.

• Place the oranges on the chopping board and cut into wedges.

• Transfer the ribs to serving plates, decorate with the orange wedges and serve with salad.

tip

★ The roasting tin will be heavy to take out of the oven so get an adult to help you and always make sure you use thick ovengloves.

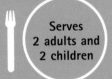

chicken dippers with salsa

③

④

④

Serves
2 adults and
2 children

equipment

colander

chopping board

small knife

fork

3 shallow bowls

liquidizer or food
processor

kitchen scissors

large frying pan

ingredients

4 boneless skinless
chicken breasts, about
625 g (1¼ lb) in total

2 eggs

2 tablespoons milk

salt and pepper

100 g (3½ oz) bread

4 tablespoons ready
grated Parmesan cheese

25 g (1 oz) butter

2 tablespoons sunflower
oil

Salsa

2 tomatoes

¼ cucumber

75 g (3 oz) sweetcorn,
defrosted if frozen

few stems fresh
coriander

what to do

1 • Put the chicken into the colander, rinse
    with cold water and drain well.

  • On the chopping board, cut the chicken
    into long, finger-like slices.

2 • Use the fork to beat the eggs, milk and
    a little salt and pepper together in a
    shallow bowl.

(3) • Tear the bread into pieces and put into the liquidizer or food processor. Blend until fine crumbs, then tip into the second shallow bowl and mix with the Parmesan.

(4) • Dip one chicken strip into the egg, then roll in the breadcrumbs. Repeat until all chicken strips are coated.

5 • For the salsa, cut the tomatoes and cucumber into tiny pieces about the size of the sweetcorn on the washed chopping board. Mix together in the third bowl.

• Snip some of the coriander into pieces with the scissors and mix 1 tablespoon into the tomato mixture.

6 • Heat the butter and oil in the frying pan, add the chicken, a few pieces at a time, until they are all added. Cook for 5–6 minutes, turning several times until evenly browned. (Cook in two batches if the pan is not very big.) Arrange on serving plates together with spoonfuls of the salsa.

tuna fishcakes

equipment

vegetable peeler

chopping board

small knife

steamer

grater

lemon squeezer

can opener

potato masher

liquidizer or food
processor

3 shallow bowls

kitchen scissors

large frying pan

fish slice

ingredients

425 g (14 oz) potatoes

125 g (4 oz) broccoli

50 g (2 oz) frozen peas

$^{1}/_{2}$ lemon

25 g (1 oz) butter

salt and pepper

2 200g (7 oz) cans
tuna in water or oil

125 g (4 oz) sliced bread

2 eggs

small bunch fresh mint

150 ml (5 fl oz) Greek or
natural yogurt

4 tablespoons sunflower
oil

what to do

1 • Peel the potatoes and cut large ones in
half on the chopping board. Put into the
base of the steamer. Cover with cold
water, bring to the boil and simmer for
10 minutes.

• Cut the broccoli into florets and the stems
into slices. Add to the top of the steamer,
cover and cook for 5 minutes. Adding peas
for the last 3 minutes

2 • Grate the rind and squeeze the juice from
the lemon.

• Drain the potatoes, put back into the dry
pan with half the lemon rind, all the juice,
the butter and a little salt and pepper.
Mash with the masher until smooth.

(3) • Open the cans of tuna and drain. Mix into the potato with the broccoli and peas.

• Spoon the mixture into eight mounds on the chopping board. Shape into rounds with floured hands when cool enough to handle.

tip

★ If you do not have a steamer, put a large colander above the pan of potatoes with a large saucepan lid or baking sheet to cover.

4 • Tear the bread into pieces, put into the food processor or liquidizer and process into fine crumbs. Tip into a shallow bowl.

• Beat the eggs in the second bowl.

• Coat the fishcakes in egg, then in breadcrumbs.

6 • Heat half the oil in the large frying pan. Add four fishcakes and fry for 5–6 minutes, turning once until golden on both sides. Cook the remaining fishcakes in the same way.

• Serve with yogurt sauce and salad.

5 • Snip the mint with the scissors. Put 4 teaspoons into the third small bowl, mix in the yogurt, remaining lemon rind and a little salt and pepper.

pass the pasta

creamy tomato and red pepper sauce

Serves
2 adults and
2 children

equipment

chopping board

knife

colander

2 saucepans, one larger
than the other

wooden spoon

can opener

ingredients

1 medium onion

400 g (13 oz) jar red
pimientos

5 pieces sun-dried
tomatoes, drained

1–2 garlic cloves

1 tablespoon olive oil

200 g (7 oz) linguine or
pasta twists

400 g (13 oz) can
chopped tomatoes

150 ml (¼ pint)
vegetable or chicken
stock

2 teaspoons caster sugar

salt and pepper

3 tablespoons double
cream (optional)

a little grated
Parmesan cheese or
shavings (see page 16)

few fresh basil leaves
(optional)

what to do

① • On the chopping board, peel and cut the
onion into small pieces.

• Crush the garlic (see page 13). Drain the
pimientos in the colander, then cut into
small squares. Thinly slice the sun-dried
tomatoes.

2 • Heat the oil in the smaller saucepan, add the onion and fry for 5 minutes, stirring from time to time with the wooden spoon, until the onion is pale golden.

3 • Meanwhile, half-fill the second saucepan with cold water, bring to the boil and add the pasta. Cook for 10 minutes, or according to the instructions on the packet, until just tender.

4 • Add the pimientos, sun-dried tomatoes and garlic to the onion. Fry for 2 more minutes, then add the canned tomatoes, stock, sugar and salt and pepper. Cook gently for 10 minutes, stirring from time to time.

5 • Drain the pasta into the colander. Tip back into the dry pan, then stir in the tomato sauce and the cream, if using.

• Toss together, then spoon into bowls and top with Parmesan cheese and basil leaves.

tuna and pasta supper

Serves
2 adults and
2 children

ingredients

150 g (5 oz) small pasta
  shapes, such as fusilli,
  shells or orzo

1 courgette

1 lemon

4 tablespoons olive oil

3 teaspoons pesto

salt and pepper

1 orange pepper

150 g (5 oz) cherry
  tomatoes

200 g (7 oz) can tuna
  in water or oil

small bunch fresh basil,
  parsley or chives
  (optional)

125 g (4 oz) sweetcorn,
  defrosted if frozen

(3)

equipment

saucepan

chopping board

small knife

lemon squeezer

serving bowl

fork

sieve or colander

can opener

kitchen scissors

what to do

1 • Half-fill the saucepan with water, bring
  to the boil, add the pasta and cook for
  8 minutes, or according to the instructions
  on the packer, until just tender.

  • Meanwhile, on the chopping board, cut
  the stalk off the courgette, then cut the
  rest into small cubes. Add to the pasta for
  the last 2 minutes of the cooking time.

2 • Halve the lemon, squeeze the juice and put
  into the serving bowl with the oil, pesto and
  salt and pepper. Fork everything together.

(3) • Drain the pasta and courgette into the
  sieve or colander and drain well. Add to
  the bowl and toss in the dressing.

(4)

(4) • On the chopping board, cut the pepper in half down from the green stalk to the bottom. Cut away the white core and stem, then scrape away the seeds. Cut the flesh into small squares.

• Halve the tomatoes.

• Open and drain the tuna and break it into pieces using the fork.

5 • If used, snip the herbs into small pieces with the scissors and add 4 tablespoons to the pasta.

• Add the pepper, tomatoes, herbs, tuna and sweetcorn. Mix with the pasta and dressing. Serve in small bowls.

spicy meat and bean pasta

Serves
2 adults and
2 children

equipment

chopping board

knife

vegetable peeler

3 saucepans of
different sizes

wooden spoon

measuring jug

colander

kitchen scissors

ingredients

1 medium onion

2 carrots

2 garlic cloves

1 tablespoon olive oil

500 g (1 lb) lean minced
lamb

1 teaspoon ground
cinnamon

$^1/_2$ teaspoon ground
allspice or nutmeg

400 g (13 oz) can
chopped tomatoes

300 ml ($^1/_2$ pint) lamb
stock

salt and pepper

250 g (8 oz) campania,
fusilli or rigatoni pasta

100 g ($3^1/_2$ oz) green
beans

100 g ($3^1/_2$ oz) frozen
broad beans

small bunch mixed fresh
mint and parsley

what to do

(1) • On the chopping board, peel and cut the
onion into small pieces.

• Peel and cut the carrots into small pieces.
Crush the garlic (see page 13).

(2) • Heat the oil in the largest saucepan, add
the onion, carrot, garlic and minced lamb
and fry for 5 minutes, stirring until the
mince is evenly browned.

- Add the spices, tomatoes, measured stock and salt and pepper. Bring to the boil, breaking up the mince with a wooden spoon.

3
- Cover with a lid and simmer the mince mixture for 1 hour, stirring from time to time so that it doesn't stick to the bottom of the pan. Top up with extra stock if needed.

4
- When the mince is almost cooked, half-fill the medium saucepan with cold water. Bring to the boil, then add the pasta. Cook for 10–12 minutes, or according to the instructions on the packet, until just tender.

(5)
- Cut the green beans in half. Half-fill the small saucepan with water, add the green and broad beans. Cook for 5 minutes until just tender.

6
- Drain the pasta in the colander. Tip back into the dry pan, then stir in the mince mixture.
- Drain the beans, then return to their dry pan. Snip the herbs with the scissors and add about 3 tablespoons to the beans.
- Spoon the pasta and mince into bowls and top with the beans.

easy chicken supper

(2)

Serves
2 adults and
2 children

equipment

saucepan

chopping board

knife

frying pan

colander

ingredients

250 g (8 oz) macaroni, fusilli or small pasta quills

125 g (4 oz) mixed frozen vegetables

325 g (11 oz) boneless, skinless chicken breasts

1 garlic clove (optional)

1 tablespoon olive oil

6 tablespoons mayonnaise

salt and pepper

little grated Parmesan or Cheddar cheese, to finish (optional)

what to do

1 • Half-fill the saucepan with water and bring to the boil. Add the pasta and simmer for 10 minutes, or according to the instructions on the packet, until just tender.

• Add the frozen vegetables to the pasta for the last 2 minutes of the cooking time.

(2) • Rinse the chicken with cold water and drain. On the chopping board, cut the meat into small squares. Crush the garlic, if using (see page 13).

3 • Heat the oil in the frying pan and add the chicken and garlic. Fry for about 5 minutes, stirring from time to time until browned and cooked through.

(4)

(**4**) • Drain the pasta and vegetables into the colander.

• Tip back into the dry pan and add the mayonnaise, chicken and a little salt and pepper. Toss together, then spoon into bowls and sprinkle with a little cheese, if liked.

jumbo macaroni cheese

Serves
2 adults and
2 children

equipment

2 saucepans, one larger
than the other

balloon whisk

grater

large sieve

chopping board

potato masher

shallow ovenproof dish,
about 2 litre (3½ pint)

kitchen scissors

knife

ingredients

250 g (8 oz) pasta quills
or rigatoni

50 g (2 oz) butter

50 g (2 oz) plain flour

600 ml (1 pint) milk

200 g (7 oz) Gruyère or
Cheddar cheese

1 teaspoon Dijon mustard
(optional)

salt and pepper

200 g (7 oz) frozen
spinach, just defrosted

3 rashers rindless
back bacon

125 g (4 oz) cherry
tomatoes

what to do

1 • Set the oven to 200°C/400°F/Gas Mark 6.

• Half-fill the larger saucepan with cold water
and bring to the boil. Add the pasta and
cook for 10 minutes, or according to the
instructions on the packet, until just tender.

② • Meanwhile, heat the butter in the second
saucepan until just melted. Whisk in the
flour, then gradually mix in the milk.

• Bring the sauce to the boil, whisking all
the time, until it is smooth and thickened.
Take the pan off the heat.

3 • Grate the cheese. Keep about 4 tablespoons back for the top and whisk the rest into the sauce with the mustard, if using, and a little salt and pepper.

• Return to the heat and stir until the cheese has melted.

4 • Drain the pasta into the sieve, then stir into the sauce.

(5) • Put the spinach into the sieve and squeeze out the liquid using the potato masher. Spoon the spinach into the base of the dish and top with the pasta and sauce.

6 • Cut the bacon into strips with the scissors.

• Sprinkle the rest of the cheese, then the bacon, over the top of the pasta.

• Halve the tomatoes and arrange them around the edge of the dish.

• Cook in the centre of the oven for 20 minutes until top is golden and the spinach is hot. Spoon on to plates and serve with sprigs of watercress or salad.

breadsticks

Makes 25

equipment

large mixing bowl

pestle and mortar or
  small bowl and
  rolling pin

measuring jug

small saucepan or
  microwaveproof bowl

wooden spoon

clingfilm

knife

2 baking sheets

ovengloves

ingredients

500 g (1 lb) strong plain
  bread flour, plus extra
  for kneading

1 teaspoon salt

1 teaspoon fast-action
  dried yeast

1 teaspoon caster sugar

1 tablespoon fennel seeds

4 tablespoons sesame
  seeds

300 ml (½ pint) milk

1

what to do

1 • Put the flour, salt, yeast and sugar into the mixing bowl.

• Roughly crush the fennel seeds in the pestle and mortar, or use the small bowl and the end of the rolling pin. Add to the flour mixture with the sesame seeds.

2 • Measure and heat the milk in the small saucepan for 1 minute until warm but not hot to the touch. Alternatively, microwave for 1 minute on Full Power.

• Gradually mix the milk into the flour mixture with the wooden spoon, then use your hands to bring the mixture together to a soft but not sticky dough. Add a little extra warm water if necessary.

3 • Sprinkle the work surface with a little flour, then knead the dough (see page 15) for 5 minutes until it is smooth and elastic.

• Put back into the bowl, cover with clingfilm and leave to rise in a warm place for 45–60 minutes until it has doubled in size.

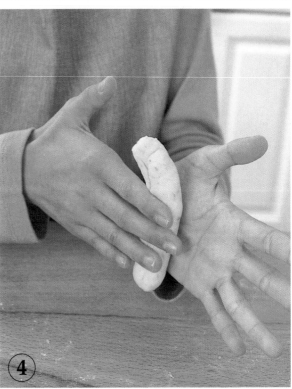

4

(4)

(4) • Knead the dough for 5 minutes until it is smooth and elastic, then cut it into 25 pieces.

• Roll each out to make a 25 cm (10 inch) long rope. Grease the baking sheets.

• Put the breadsticks slightly spaced apart on to the baking sheets. Cover with lightly oiled clingfilm and leave to rise in a warm place for 20–30 minutes until they are half as big again.

• Meanwhile, set the oven to 200°C/400°F/ Gas Mark 6.

5 • Discard the clingfilm and bake the breadsticks in the oven for 6–8 minutes until pale golden. Serve cold.

foccacia

ingredients

750 g (1½ lb) strong plain bread flour, plus extra for kneading

7 g (¼ oz) sachet fast-action dried yeast

3 teaspoons caster sugar

2 teaspoons salt

9 tablespoons olive oil

450 ml (¾ pint) warm water

6 pieces sun-dried tomatoes

few stems rosemary

few black olives, pitted

little coarse sea salt (optional)

Makes 3

equipment

large mixing bowl

large measuring jug

wooden spoon

clingfilm

kitchen scissors

2 large baking sheets

pastry brush

ovengloves

tea towel

what to do

1 • Put the flour, yeast, sugar and salt into the bowl. Add 3 tablespoons of the olive oil.

• Measure and test the water – it should feel warm but not too hot or it will kill the yeast.

• Gradually mix in the water using the wooden spoon, then mix with your hands to make a soft but not sticky dough.

② • Sprinkle the work surface with some flour, then knead the dough (see page 15) for 5 minutes until smooth and elastic.

3 • Put the dough back into the bowl, cover with clingfilm and put in a warm place for 45–60 minutes until the dough has doubled in size.

4 • Tip the risen dough out on to the work surface and knead again until smooth.

- Cut into three pieces and pat each into a rough oval, about 23 cm (9 inches) in diameter. Place on two large baking sheets that have been brushed with oil.

(5) • Make dents over each loaf, by pressing the end of the wooden spoon into the dough.

- Snip the sun-dried tomatoes and rosemary into pieces with the scissors. Press into the holes in the bread along with the olives.

- Leave to rise for a second time in a warm place for about 20–30 minutes until about half as big again.

6 • Meanwhile, set the oven to 200°C/ 400°F/Gas Mark 6.

7 • Spoon 1 tablespoon of olive oil over each piece of bread and sprinkle with coarse salt, if using.

- Bake in the oven for 15 minutes until the foccacia are golden brown and sound hollow when tapped with your fingers – get adult help for this. Spoon the rest of the oil over the bread.

- Serve warm or cold, torn into strips, with soup or salad.

tip

 Yeast comes in three kinds – fresh, dried yeast that must be soaked in warm liquid before use, and the fast acting kind used in this recipe and in bread-making machines.

quick cheese and chive bread

(2)

Makes 6
pieces

equipment

baking sheet

pastry brush

large mixing bowl

small knife

electric mixer (optional)

grater

kitchen scissors

cup or mug

fork or wooden spoon

ovengloves

ingredients

250 g (8 oz) self-raising
flour, plus extra for
kneading

salt and pepper

40 g (1½ oz) butter

125 g (4 oz) Cheddar
cheese

small bunch fresh
chives

1 egg

150 ml (¼ pint) milk

1 teaspoon Dijon mustard

what to do

1 • Set the oven to 200°C/400°F/Gas Mark 6.

• Brush the baking sheet with a little oil.

(2) • Put the flour and salt and pepper into the
large mixing bowl.

• Cut the butter into pieces and add to
bowl, then rub in with your fingertips or
an electric mixer until the mixture looks
like fine crumbs (see page 15).

3 • Grate the cheese coarsely and snip the
chives into pieces with the scissors. Add
the cheese and about 4 tablespoons of
chives to the bowl and mix together.

(4)

- Beat the egg in the cup or mug and add all but about 2 teaspoons of the egg to the flour mixture.

- Add the mustard, then gradually mix in the milk to make a soft but not sticky ball with the fork or wooden spoon.

(4) • Sprinkle the work surface with a little flour, then tip the dough on to it. Knead until smooth, then pat into a circle about 18 cm (7 inches) or a little bigger than your hand across.

- Cut into six segments and put slightly spaced apart on the baking sheet.

5 • Brush the tops of the rolls with the remaining egg.

- Bake in the centre of the oven for 15 minutes until well risen and golden. Serve warm or cold, split and buttered on their own or with bowls of hot soup.

Makes 12

equipment

roasting tin, 18 x 28 cm (7 x 11 inch)

pastry brush

large mixing bowl

measuring jug

wooden spoon

rolling pin

small bowl

knife

grater

clingfilm

ovengloves

tea towel

cheesy spirals

ingredients

500 g (1 lb) strong plain bread flour, plus extra for kneading

1 teaspoon salt

2 teaspoons fast-action dried yeast

2 teaspoons caster sugar

300 ml (½ pint) warm water

Filling

3 teaspoons pesto

3 tablespoons tomato ketchup

2 tablespoons olive oil

2 tomatoes

salt and pepper

150 g (5 oz) Cheddar, mozzarella or Gruyère cheese

what to do

1 • Brush the roasting tin with a little oil.

  • Put the flour, salt, yeast and sugar in the large mixing bowl.

  • Measure and test the water – it should feel warm but not hot. (If it is too hot the yeast will be killed.)

  • Gradually mix water into the flour with the wooden spoon, then shape with your hands into a soft but not sticky ball.

2 • Sprinkle the work surface with a little flour, then tip the dough on to it. Knead (see page 15) for 10 minutes until smooth and elastic.

  • Roll out the dough to a rectangle about 40 x 25 cm (16 x 10 inches).

③

④

5 • Remove the clingfilm from the bread. Bake in the oven for 20–25 minutes until well risen and golden and the bread sounds hollow when tapped with your fingers – get adult help for this. Leave to cool in tin. Serve warm or cold.

③ • For the filling, mix the pesto, ketchup and oil in the small bowl, then spread over the dough.

• Chop the tomatoes finely and sprinkle over the pesto mixture.

• Grate the cheese and sprinkle over.

④ • Roll up the dough, starting with one of the long edges, then cut into 12 thick slices.

• Arrange, side by side with cut side uppermost, in the roasting tin. If spirals look squashed, open out with the tip of a knife. Brush a piece of clingfilm with a little oil, then put oil side down on the bread.

• Leave in a warm place for 45–60 minutes until well risen.

• Meanwhile, set the oven to 200°C/400°F/ Gas Mark 6.

pizza mania

③

Makes 4

equipment

large mixing bowl
measuring jug
wooden spoon
small knife
rolling pin
2 baking sheets
chopping board
ovengloves

ingredients

375 g (12 oz) strong white bread flour, plus extra for kneading

salt and pepper

1 teaspoon fast-action dried yeast

1 teaspoon caster sugar

250 ml (8 fl oz) warm water

Toppings
200 g (7 oz) pizza sauce or passata topping

75 g (3 oz) courgette

50 g (2 oz) sweetcorn, defrosted if frozen

40 g (1¹/₂ oz) thinly sliced salami or ham

150 g (5 oz) mozzarella cheese

2 teaspoons pesto sauce or a few fresh basil leaves

few pitted olives (optional)

what to do

1   • Put the flour, salt and pepper, yeast and sugar into the large mixing bowl. Measure and test the temperature of the water – it should feel just warm. If it is too hot the yeast will be killed.

   • Gradually mix in the water with the wooden spoon to make a soft but not sticky dough.

2   • Sprinkle the work surface with a little flour, then knead the dough (see page 15) for 10 minutes until smooth and elastic.

④

3 • Cut the dough into four, roll each into a rough circle about 18 cm (7 inches) in diameter and put them on to the (ungreased) baking sheets.

4 • Spread each pizza with the pizza sauce or passata.

• On the chopping board, trim the stalk off the courgette, then cut the rest into small cubes. Sprinkle over the pizzas with the sweetcorn.

5 • Cut the salami or ham into strips. Drain and thinly slice the cheese. Arrange on the pizzas. Dot the pesto thinly over the cheese or add the basil leaves. Add the olives, if using.

6 • Leave the pizzas to rise in a warm place for 30 minutes until the bread is puffy around the edges.

• Meanwhile, set the oven to 220°C/425°F/ Gas Mark 7.

7 • Bake the pizzas in the oven for 8–10 minutes until the edges are golden. Serve warm with salad.

tips

★ To make pizzas into calzone, simply fold the pizza in half and seal the edges well with water to make a pizza-style parcel.

★ For alternative toppings, mix and match your favourite combinations.

cheesy hearts

Makes 25

equipment

small knife

large mixing bowl

electric mixer (optional)

grater

fork

rolling pin

heart–shaped biscuit
  cutter

2 baking sheets

small bowl

pastry brush

ovengloves

ingredients

175 g (6 oz) butter

250 g (8 oz) plain flour,
  plus extra for kneading

salt and pepper

175 g (6 oz) Gruyère or
  Cheddar cheese

2 egg yolks

1 whole egg

what to do

1 • Set the oven to 200°C/400°F/Gas Mark 6.

• Cut the butter into pieces and add to the large mixing bowl with the flour and salt and pepper.

• Rub in the butter with your fingertips or an electric mixer until the mixture looks like fine crumbs (see page 15).

2 • Grate the cheese, then stir three-quarters into the bowl with the egg yolks. Mix with the fork, then shape the dough into a ball with your hands.

3 • Sprinkle the work surface with a little flour. Knead the ball of dough until it is smooth, then roll it out until it is 5 mm (¼ inch) thick.

4 • Cut out hearts or other shapes and put the biscuits spaced slightly apart on the (ungreased) baking sheets.

• Squeeze all the trimmings together, then roll out and continue stamping and kneading until all the mixture is used up.

5 • Beat the whole egg in the small bowl and brush the biscuits with it using the pastry brush. Sprinkle with the remaining grated cheese.

• Bake in the oven for 8–10 minutes until golden. Leave to cool on the sheets.

tips

★ The biscuits could be sprinkled with sesame or poppy seeds before baking or left plain if preferred.

★ If you don't have any biscuit cutters, cut squares, triangles or strips instead using a small knife.

cheese and courgette muffins

Makes 12

equipment

12-hole muffin tin
12 paper muffin cases
large mixing bowl
knife
grater
fork
large spoon
ovengloves

③

ingredients

300 g (10 oz) self-raising flour	1 courgette, about 200 g (7 oz)
salt and pepper	150 ml (5 fl oz) pot natural yogurt
3 teaspoons baking powder	3 tablespoons olive oil
75 g (3 oz) grated Parmesan cheese	3 eggs
	3 tablespoons milk

what to do

1 • Set the oven to 200°C/400°F/Gas Mark 6.

• Line the muffin tin with the paper cases.

2 • Put the flour, salt and pepper, baking powder and Parmesan cheese into the large mixing bowl.

③ • Cut the stalk off the courgette, then coarsely grate it. Add the courgette to the bowl with the yogurt, oil, eggs and milk. Fork together until just mixed.

③

(4) • Spoon the muffin mixture into the paper cases, filling each case two-thirds full.

• Bake them in the centre of the oven for 18–20 minutes until well risen and golden brown. Serve warm or cold with bowls of hot soup or a little butter for a snack.

tips

★ Muffins freeze well in a plastic bag. Microwave from frozen one at a time or defrost them at room temperature and add to lunch boxes.

★ Try mixing a little grated carrot in place of some of the courgette for a change.

what's for pudding?

'take 5' fruit salad

ingredients

1 galia or ogen melon

1 small pineapple

2 kiwi fruit

125 g (4 oz) green
  seedless grapes

2 limes

2 tablespoons runny
  honey

Serves 6

equipment

chopping board

large and small knives

dessert spoon

serving bowl

small round biscuit cutter

vegetable peeler

grater

lemon squeezer

what to do

(1) • Put the melon on the chopping board and carefully cut it in half with the large knife. Scoop out the seeds with the spoon and cut the melon into four wedges.

• Using the same spoon, scoop the melon away from the skin, cut it into cubes and put them into the serving bowl.

2 • With the large knife, cut the green top off the pineapple and put it on one side – get adult help for this. Cut the pineapple into thick crosswise slices and cut away the prickly skin.

• Using the small biscuit cutter, cut away the round hard core from the centre and discard. Cut the fruit into pieces and add to the melon.

(1)

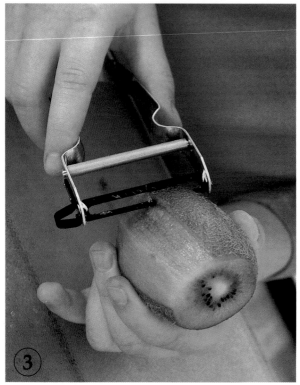

(3)

92

(3) • Peel the skin off the kiwi fruit with the vegetable peeler and cut the flesh into squares. Halve the grapes and add both to the melon.

4 • Finely grate the rind from the limes and cut them in half.

• Squeeze out the lime juice and add to the fruit, making sure you do not add the pips.

• Spoon the honey over, then mix all the fruits together and serve.

93

mini raspberry pancakes

Serves
2 adults and
2 children

equipment

mixing bowl

whisk

pastry brush

frying pan or griddle

large metal spoon

palette knife or fish slice

plate

ingredients

200 g (7 oz) self-raising
  flour

25 g (1 oz) caster sugar

1 teaspoon baking
  powder

1 teaspoon vanilla
  essence

2 eggs

250 ml (8 fl oz) milk

little sunflower oil,
  for cooking

little butter,
  for spreading

maple syrup, to serve

125 g (4 oz) fresh or
  frozen raspberries

what to do

1 • Put the flour, sugar, baking powder, vanilla
  essence and eggs into the bowl.

• Gradually whisk in the milk, little by little,
  until the mixture is smooth and all the
  milk has been added.

2 • Brush a little oil over the base of the large
  frying pan or griddle.

• Heat for 1–2 minutes, then add large
  spoonfuls of the pancake mixture to the
  pan, leaving space between each spoonful
  so that they don't all join up to make one
  big pancake!

3 • Cook the pancakes for about 1 minute on the first side or until bubbles appear on the top of each pancake.

• Turn over the pancakes with the palette knife or fish slice and cook the other side for about 1 minute until golden. From time to time lift to check if they are browned.

4 • Lift the cooked pancakes on to the plate. Continue making pancakes in the same way until all the mixture is used up.

5 • Spread the pancakes with butter and stack on to serving plates. Drizzle with maple syrup and sprinkle with raspberries.

tip

★ For a simple treat, these pancakes are delicious spread with chocolate spread, or a little butter and jam or honey.

chocolate puddle pudding

Serves 4–6

equipment

2 mixing bowls, one larger than the other

measuring jug

wooden spoon

ovenproof glass soufflé dish or pie dish, 1.2 litre (2 pint)

baking sheet

electric mixer (optional)

ovengloves

small sieve

ingredients

Sauce

2 tablespoons cocoa powder

50 g (2 oz) soft light brown sugar

250 ml (8 fl oz) boiling water

Pudding

75 g (3 oz) soft margarine or softened butter

75 g (3 oz) soft light brown sugar

65 g (2½ oz) self-raising flour

3 tablespoons cocoa powder

3 eggs

little icing sugar, to finish

½ teaspoon baking powder

what to do

1 • Set the oven to 180°C/350°F/Gas Mark 4.

• To make the sauce, put the cocoa and sugar into the smaller bowl and use the wooden spoon to mix in a little of the measured boiling water to make a smooth paste. Gradually mix in the rest of the boiling water.

(2) • To make the pudding, rub a little of the margarine or butter all over the base and sides of the cooking dish and stand the dish on the baking sheet.

• Put all the other ingredients, except the icing sugar, into the second bowl and beat together with the wooden spoon or electric mixer until smooth.

tip

★ The deeper the dish, the longer it will take for the pudding to cook.

3 • Spoon the pudding mixture into the dish, spread the top level, then pour the cocoa sauce over the top.

• Bake in the centre of the oven for 15 minutes until the sauce has sunk to the bottom of the dish and the pudding is well risen.

• To finish, sift a little icing sugar on to the pudding and serve with scoops of vanilla ice cream or a little pouring cream.

easy orange cheesecake

Serves 6

equipment

plastic bag

rolling pin

small saucepan

wooden spoon

round springform tin
20 cm (8 inch)

can opener

sieve

two medium mixing
bowls

zester or grater

lemon squeezer

hand or electric whisk

metal spoon

thin-bladed knife

ingredients

150 g (5 oz) digestive
biscuits

50 g (2 oz) butter

2 tablespoons golden
syrup

312 g (10½ oz) can
mandarin oranges in
natural juice

250 g (8 oz) tub
mascarpone cheese

150 g (5 oz) virtually
fat-free fromage frais

50 g (2 oz) caster sugar

1 small orange

1 lime

150 ml (¼ pint) double
cream

what to do

1 • Put the biscuits into the plastic bag, seal
and bash with the rolling pin until the
biscuits become fine crumbs.

• Heat the butter and syrup in the saucepan
until melted, stir in the biscuit crumbs
with the wooden spoon and mix well.

② • Tip the crumb mixture into the base of the
springform tin and press flat with the end
of the rolling pin.

3 • Open the can of mandarin oranges and
tip into the sieve to drain off the juice.

• Arrange about three-quarters of them
over the crumbs in the tin. Keep the rest
for decorating.

4 • Put the mascarpone cheese into one of the mixing bowls and mix with the wooden spoon to soften it. Stir in the fromage frais and sugar.

• Take the rind off the orange and lime with the zester or the fine holes on the grater, then cut the fruits in half and squeeze out the juice. Stir the rind and juice into the cheese mixture.

5 • Use the hand or an electric whisk to whip the cream in the second bowl until it thickens and becomes soft swirls.

• Gently fold into the cheese mixture.

6 • Pour the mixture into the tin and make soft wave-like shapes over the top with the back of the metal spoon.

• Decorate with the remaining mandarins and chill the cheesecake in the refrigerator for 4 hours or longer if you have time.

7 • To serve, run a thin-bladed knife around the edge of the cheesecake. Unclip the tin and transfer the cheesecake to a serving plate.

99

nectarine and coconut crumble

equipment

colander

chopping board

small knife

pie dish, 1.2 litre (2 pint)

mixing bowl

ovengloves

ingredients

750 g (1½ lb) ripe nectarines

75 g (3 oz) caster sugar

50 g (2 oz) butter

100 g (3½ oz) plain flour

50 g (2 oz) desiccated coconut

what to do

① • Set the oven to 180°C/350°F/Gas Mark 4.

  • Wash the nectarines in cold water and drain in the colander. On the chopping board, cut each one in half, take out the stone and cut the fruit into thick slices.

2 • Tip the fruit into the bottom of the pie dish and sprinkle with 2 tablespoons of the sugar.

③ • Put the rest of the sugar into the mixing bowl. Cut the butter into small squares. Add the butter and flour to the bowl.

  • Rub the butter into the flour between your fingertips to make tiny crumbs (see page 15). Stir in the coconut.

4 • Spoon the coconut crumble over the nectarines.

• Cook in the centre of the oven for 25 minutes until the crumble is golden brown. Serve warm with scoops of vanilla ice cream or pouring cream.

tip

★ Check the crumble after 10 minutes. Some ovens are hotter than others and because coconut makes the crumble brown quickly, you may need to cover the top with foil so that it doesn't become too dark before it is cooked.

strawberry sundae jellies

Serves
2 adults and
2 children

ingredients

135 g (4½ oz)
strawberry jelly tablet

250 g (8 oz) fresh
strawberries

200 g (7 oz) fromage
frais

2 tablespoons caster sugar

extra small strawberries,
to decorate

equipment

kitchen scissors

large measuring jug

metal spoon

sieve

liquidizer, food
processor or a plate
and fork

four jelly moulds
150 ml (¼ pint)

mixing bowl

teaspoon

what to do

1 • Cut the jelly into pieces with the scissors
and put into the bottom of the large
measuring jug.

• Pour on 300 ml (½ pint) of boiling water
and mix with the metal spoon until the
jelly has melted. Leave to cool.

2 • Rinse the strawberries with cold water,
drain and take out the green tops. Purée
the strawberries in the liquidizer or food
processor or mash on the plate using
the fork.

• Stir into the jelly with the fromage frais
and sugar and mix until smooth.

3 • Pour the jelly mixture into four domed or fancy shaped jelly moulds.

• Chill in the refrigerator for 4 hours, or longer if you have time, until set.

4 • To turn the jellies out, dip each mould into the mixing bowl, half-filled with hot water from the kettle – you may need adult help for this.

• Count to 10, then carefully take the jellies out of the water, and turn upside down on to serving plates. Hold the plate and the mould and jerk to release.

(5) • Carefully take off the moulds and top each with a halved strawberry.

tip

★ Try making these sundae jelllies with different flavoured jelly tablets and top them with your favourite fruit.

warm summer fruit trifle

Serves 6

equipment

ovenproof soufflé or
pie dish, 1.2 litre
(2 pint)

can opener

tablespoon

large mixing bowl

electric whisk

ovengloves

ingredients

100 g (3½ oz) trifle
sponges, plain sponge,
Madeira cake or jam
Swiss roll

3 tablespoons orange
juice, freshly squeezed
or from a carton

375 g (12 oz) frozen
mixed summer fruits,
just defrosted

425 g (14 oz) can
custard

3 egg whites

75 g (3 oz) caster sugar

what to do

1 • Set the oven to 170°C/325°F/Gas Mark 3.

• Crumble the sponge into the base of the
ovenproof serving dish. Drizzle the orange
juice over the sponge. Add the mixed fruits.

• Spoon the can of custard over the top.

2 • Put the egg whites into the large bowl.
With an electric whisk, whisk until the
eggs fill the bowl and the bowl can be
turned upside down without them falling
out! Gradually whisk in the sugar, a
spoonful at a time.

• Whisk for a minute or two more once all
the sugar has been added until the egg
mixture looks smooth and glossy.

104

3 • Spoon the egg mixture over the top of the custard and leave the top in large swirls.

• Cook in the centre of the oven for 20 minutes until the meringue is golden brown on the top and all the trifle layers are heated through.

tip

★ Lightly cooked apples and blackberries or a can of cherry pie filling make delicious trifle fillings.

peach puff pies

Makes 12

ingredients

1 sheet ready-rolled puff
pastry from a 425 g
(14 oz) pack of two

1 egg

2 ripe peaches

2 tablespoons strawberry
or apricot jam

200 g (7 oz) crème
fraîche

125 g (4 oz) raspberries,
defrosted if frozen

little icing sugar

equipment

pastry brush

baking sheet

small knife

fork

2 small bowls

chopping board

tablespoon

ovengloves

what to do

1 • Set the oven to 200°C/400°F/Gas Mark 6.

• Using the pastry brush, brush the baking
tray with a little oil.

2 • Unroll the puff pastry sheet and cut it into
12 pieces.

• Peel off the paper and place the pastry
squares, slightly spaced apart, on the
baking sheet.

3 • Beat the egg with the fork in one of the
small bowls and use to brush over the
pastry.

4 • Wash the peaches, place on the chopping
board and cut into small pieces, discarding
the stones.

②

④

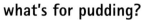

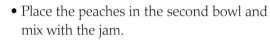

what's for pudding?

- Place the peaches in the second bowl and mix with the jam.

- Divide the peach and jam mixture among the pastry squares.

5 • Bake the peach pies in the centre of the oven for 10 minutes until well risen and golden.

- Leave to cool, then top the pies with spoonfuls of crème fraîche and the raspberries. Dust with icing sugar and serve.

watermelon lollies

Serves 6

equipment

large metal spoon

food processor or
  liquidizer

sieve

large bowl

large jug

grater

lemon squeezer

plastic ice lolly mould

freezer

bowl

ingredients

625 g (1¼ lb) wedge of
  watermelon

2 limes

150 ml (¼ pint) apple
  juice

2 tablespoons caster
  sugar

what to do

1 • Using the large metal spoon, scoop the red melon flesh and black seeds away from the green skin and into the food processor or liquidizer.

2 • Blend briefly so that the fruit is puréed but the seeds are still whole.

 • Tip the mixture into the sieve set over the large bowl and press the red melon flesh through the sieve with the metal spoon, leaving the seeds behind in the sieve.

4 • Finely grate the rind of the limes and add to the melon purée. Cut the limes in half and squeeze out the juice. Stir into the melon purée with the apple juice and sugar.

(5) • Pour the melon mixture into sections of the ice lolly mould. Add the tops.

• Freeze for 4 hours, or longer if you have time, until frozen solid.

6 • To take the lollies out of the moulds, dip the plastic mould into a bowl of just boiled water from the kettle – you may need adult help with this. Count to 10, then lift each lolly and top out of mould and serve.

tip

★ Use this same idea to make papaya, mango or peach lollies, but remove the seeds or stones before puréeing.

strawberry sherbet

Serves 6–8

equipment

medium saucepan

sieve

food processor or
  liquidizer

mixing bowl

balloon whisk

ice cream machine or
  plastic freezerproof
  container

freezer

fork

ingredients

175 g (6 oz) caster sugar

150 ml (¼ pint) water

500 g (1 lb) strawberries

500 g (1 lb) virtually
  fat-free fromage frais

8 waffle ice cream cones

what to do

1 • Put the sugar and water into the saucepan
and cook gently until the sugar has
dissolved.

• Boil for 1 minute, then turn off the heat –
get adult help for this because sugar syrup
gets very hot.

2 • Rinse the strawberries with cold water,
drain in the sieve and take out the
green tops.

• Purée the strawberries in the liquidizer or
food processor until smooth. (There is no
need to sieve.) Transfer to the bowl.

③ • Whisk the fromage frais into the puréed
fruit, then gradually mix in the cooled
sugar syrup.

• Pour the mixture into the pre-cooled ice
cream machine and churn for about 45
minutes or until it is thick.

- Alternatively, pour the strawberry mixture into the plastic container and freeze for 3 hours.

(4) • Scoop the semi-frozen sherbet from the plastic box into the food processor or liquidizer and blend until smooth.

Alternatively, use the fork to beat the sherbet while it is still in the plastic container.

- Put back into the freezer for 3 more hours or until firm enough to scoop. Serve in ice cream cones.

tip

★ To decorate some plain ice cream cones, dip the tops into 100 g (3½ oz) melted white or dark chocolate and then, before the chocolate sets, sprinkle it with pastel coloured sugar strands or grated chocolate. Leave to harden, then add the sherbet or ice cream.

Serves 6

apple snow

ingredients

5 large dessert apples

1 lemon, juice only

125 g (4 oz) caster sugar

300 ml (½ pint) water

few drops green food colouring (optional)

jelly beans, to decorate

equipment

chopping board

small sharp knife

vegetable peeler

medium saucepan with lid

lemon squeezer

liquidizer or food processor, or sieve and bowl

shallow stainless steel or plastic freezerproof container

freezer

fork

what to do

(1) • On the chopping board, cut the apples into quarters, then cut away the cores and peel off the skins using a vegetable peeler.

• Thickly slice the apples.

2 • Put the apple slices into the saucepan.

• Cut the lemon in half, squeeze the juice, then add to the pan with the sugar and water. Cover with the lid and gently cook for 5 minutes until the apples are very soft.

(3) • Leave the mixture to cool, then purée in the liquidizer or food processor with a few drops of green food colouring, if using.

• Or press through a sieve into a bowl.

• Pour the mixture into the shallow stainless steel or plastic container so that the apple mixture is only about 2.5 cm (1 inch) deep.

• Freeze for 2 hours until the edges of the mixture are icy.

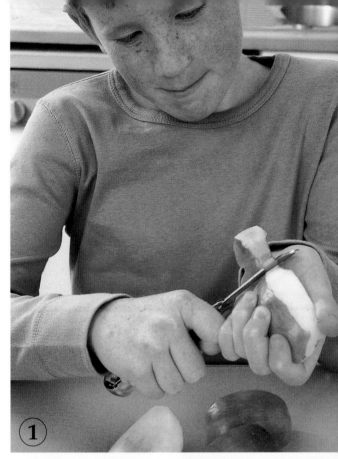

(1)

(3)

4 • Beat the mixture with the fork until the icy edges become smooth.

• Freeze again for 30 minutes, then beat with the fork again.

• Continue beating and freezing four more times until the mixture looks like snow. It should take about 2 hours in all.

5 • Spoon the iced apple into bowls and decorate with jelly beans.

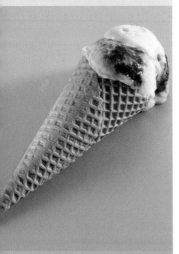

raspberry ripple

Serves 6

equipment

large mixing bowl

hand-held or electric whisk

can opener

large spoon

2 plastic containers, one larger than the other

freezer

fork or food processor

small knife

chopping board

ingredients

450 ml (³/₄ pint) double cream

405 g (13 oz) can sweetened condensed milk

1 teaspoon vanilla essence

4 tablespoons soft set raspberry jam

2 peaches and a few fresh or frozen raspberries, to decorate

ice cream cone, to serve

what to do

1 • Pour the cream into the mixing bowl. Whisk with the hand-held or electric whisk until beginning to thicken and making soft, wave-like swirls.

2 • Open the can of condensed milk and stir into the cream with the vanilla essence. Pour the mixture into the larger plastic container.

   • Freeze for 3 hours until semi-frozen.

③ • Beat the ice cream with the fork to break up ice crystals or use the food processor, if preferred.

   • Scoop one-third into the second plastic container and dot with half the jam. Cover with a second layer of ice cream, the rest of the jam, then the last of the ice cream.

- Run a knife through the layers to make the marbled effect.

4 • Return the ice cream to the freezer and chill for at least 3 hours or until hard enough to scoop.

5 • Scoop ice cream into cones and serve.

tip

★ Homemade ice cream is more difficult to scoop than bought ice cream, especially if it has been in the freezer for a couple of days. Therefore, take out of the freezer about 15 minutes before you need it, so it can soften before scooping.

chunky monkey cookies

Makes 18

equipment

large mixing bowl
medium knife
electric mixer (optional)
cup or mug
chopping board
2–3 baking sheets
dessertspoon
ovengloves
palette knife
wire cooling rack

ingredients

200 g (7 oz) plain flour

1 teaspoon bicarbonate of soda

125 g (4 oz) caster sugar

125 g (4 oz) butter

1 egg

1 tablespoon milk

150 g (5 oz) white chocolate

75 g (3 oz) glacé cherries

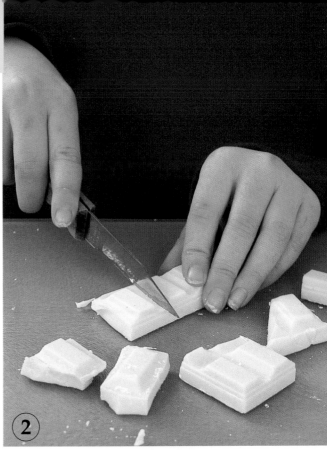

(2)

what you do

1 • Set the oven to 180°C/350°F/Gas Mark 4.

• Put the flour, bicarbonate of soda and sugar into the bowl and mix together.

• Cut the butter into small pieces and add to the bowl. Rub in the butter with your fingertips or an electric mixer until the mixture looks like fine crumbs (see page 15).

(2) • Beat together the egg and milk in the cup or mug. Chop the chocolate and cherries into rough pieces on the chopping board, then add all four ingredients to the bowl and mix together.

(3)

(3) • Grease the baking sheets. Drop heaped dessertspoonfuls of cookie mixture, well spaced apart, on to the baking sheets.

• Bake in the oven for 8–12 minutes until lightly browned. Leave for 2 minutes to harden, then transfer with the palette knife to the wire cooling rack.

tip

★ Mix and match the flavourings depending on your favourites and what you can find in the cupboard. Dark chocolate instead of white or ready-to-eat dried apricots could be added instead of the cherries, or use sultanas and raisins to replace the white chocolate to make an all-fruit version.

fruity crumble squares

Makes 16

equipment

small knife

large mixing bowl

electric food mixer (optional)

shallow square baking tin, 20 cm (8 inches)

kitchen scissors

grater

ovengloves

ingredients

175 g (6 oz) butter, at room temperature

250 g (8 oz) plain flour

2 tablespoons cornflour

75 g (3 oz) caster sugar

100 g (3½ oz) exotic ready-to-eat dried fruits, or just apricots

1 small dessert apple

little icing sugar

what to do

1 • Set the oven to 180°C/350°F/Gas Mark 4.

• Cut the butter into pieces with the knife and put into the large bowl with the flour, cornflour and sugar.

• Rub in the butter with your fingertips or an electric mixer until the mixture looks like fine crumbs (see page 15). Measure out 125 g (4 oz) of the crumbs and reserve for later.

2 • Squeeze the rest of the crumbs together with your hands to make a ball, then press the mixture into the base of the ungreased baking tin using your knuckles.

3 • Cut the dried fruit into pieces with the scissors.

• Grate the apple (still with its skin on) over the shortbread mixture in the tin and throw away the core.

• Top with the snipped dried fruits. Sprinkle with the saved crumb mixture.

4 • Bake in the centre of the oven for 30 minutes until the top is lightly browned.

• Leave to cool in the tin for 15 minutes, then cut into 12 pieces and leave to cool completely.

• Decorate with a litle sifted icing sugar.

orange meltaways

Makes 20

equipment

grater

chopping board

knife

lemon squeezer

food processor or large
    mixing bowl and
    wooden spoon

large star piping tube
    and nylon piping bag

jug

2–3 baking sheets

small bowl

fine sieve

metal spoon

small chopping board
    and knife

ovengloves

wire cooling rack

palette knife

120

ingredients

1 small orange

175 g (6 oz) butter

200 g (7 oz) plain flour

150 g (5 oz) icing sugar

few peeled pistachio
    nuts, orange rind or
    glacé cherries, to
    decorate

what to do

1 • Set the oven to 160°C/325°F/Gas Mark 3.

   • Finely grate the rind of the orange. On the
    chopping board, cut the fruit in half and
    squeeze the juice.

2 • Cut the butter into large pieces and put
    into the food processor or large bowl with
    the orange rind, 1 tablespoon of the juice,
    the flour and 50 g (2 oz) of the icing sugar.

   • Beat the ingredients together until
    smooth, soft and completely lump free.

③ • Put the large star tube into the bottom of
    the nylon piping bag, stand it in the jug,
    then spoon in the biscuit mixture.

   • Squeeze the mixture down to the bottom
    of the bag, then pipe rings, about 6 cm
    (2½ inches) wide, on to the ungreased
    baking sheets.

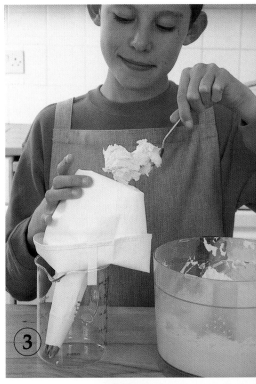

③

③

4 • Bake in the centre of the oven for 10 minutes until pale golden.

• Meanwhile, sift the rest of the icing sugar into the small bowl using the fine sieve and metal spoon.

• Stir in 3–4 teaspoons orange juice to make a smooth, thin icing.

• Finely chop the pistachios or cherries on the small chopping board.

5 • Lift the hot biscuits on to the wire cooling rack using the palette knife.

• Brush the icing over the top. Sprinkle the pistachio nuts or cherries and orange rind over the biscuits and leave to cool.

tips

★ These little biscuits can also be piped into stars or S shapes.

★ Piping biscuits is much easier to do than it might look, but if you would rather not use a piping bag, roll the mixture into small balls with floured hands and arrange them on baking sheets instead.

Makes 12

equipment

muffin paper cases

12–hole muffin tin

large mixing bowl

wooden spoon or electric
   mixer

small bowl

fork

sieve

plate

dessertspoon

chopping board

small knife

ovengloves

double chocolate muffins

(2)

ingredients

125 g (4 oz) soft
   margarine

125 g (4 oz) caster sugar

3 eggs

1 teaspoon vanilla
   essence

5 tablespoons milk

200 g (7 oz) self-raising
   flour

15 g ($^1/_2$ oz) cocoa
   powder

75 g (3 oz) milk or dark
   chocolate

what to do

1 • Set the oven to 190°C/375°F/Gas Mark 5.

• Place the paper cases in the sections in
   the muffin tin.

• Beat the soft margarine and sugar together
   in the large bowl with the wooden spoon or
   electric mixer until light and fluffy.

(2) • Beat the eggs, vanilla essence and milk
   together in the small bowl using the fork.

• Sift the flour and cocoa on to the plate.

3 • Beat a little of the egg mixture into the
   margarine mixture, then add a little of the
   cocoa mixture. Continue adding in this
   way until all of it has been mixed in.

(4)

4 • Spoon the mixture into the paper cases until each one is half-full.

• Cut the chocolate into 12 squares on a chopping board and put one square into each muffin case.

5 • Spoon the rest of the muffin mixture into the paper cases.

• Bake the muffins in the oven for 15–18 minutes until well risen and the tops are cracked.

• Cool slightly and serve while still warm so that chocolate is still gooey in the middle.

gingersnaps

Makes 30

equipment

3 baking sheets

pastry brush

medium saucepan

wooden spoon

sieve

teaspoon

ovengloves

palette knife

wire cooling rack

ingredients

100 g (3½ oz) butter

100 g (3½ oz) light
brown sugar

100 g (3½ oz) golden
syrup

225 g (7½ oz) plain
flour

1 teaspoon bicarbonate
of soda

1 teaspoon ground ginger

what to do

1 • Set the oven to 180°C/350°F/Gas Mark 4.

• Brush the baking sheets with a little oil
using the pastry brush.

• Put the butter, sugar and syrup into the
saucepan and heat gently, stirring with a
wooden spoon, until the butter has
melted. Leave to cool for 5 minutes.

2 • Sift the flour, bicarbonate of soda and
ginger into the saucepan. Mix with the
wooden spoon until a smooth soft dough.

3 • Take teaspoons of the mixture and dot
over the work surface. Cool slightly, roll
each spoonful in your hand to make a
smooth, round ball, then put them on to
the baking sheets, slightly spaced apart.

②

③

(3)

4 • Bake the biscuits in the oven for 8–10 minutes until the tops have cracked and are just beginning to brown.

• Cool on the baking sheets for 2 minutes. Loosen with the palette knife and transfer to the wire cooling rack.

5 • Pack the gingersnaps into small boxes lined with waxed or greaseproof paper.

Easter chocolate nests

Makes 12

equipment

12 paper cake or medium muffin cases

12–hole cake or muffin tin

fine sieve

mixing bowl

wooden spoon or electric mixer

dessertspoon

oven gloves

butter knife

ingredients

15 g (½ oz) cocoa powder

125 g (4 oz) soft margarine or butter, at room temperature

125 g (4 oz) caster sugar

100 g (3½ oz) self-raising flour

2 eggs

4 tablespoons chocolate spread

3 crumbly chocolate bars

200 g (7 oz) mini eggs

few Easter chick decorations (optional)

what to do

1 • Set the oven to 180°C/350°F/Gas Mark 4.

• Place the paper cases into the sections of the muffin tin.

2 • Put the cocoa powder, margarine or butter, sugar, flour, cocoa and eggs into the bowl.

• Beat together with the wooden spoon or electric mixer until smooth.

(3) • Spoon the mixture into the paper cases so that they are half-filled.

• Bake in the centre of the oven for 12–15 minutes until well risen and the tops spring back when pressed lightly with a finger. Leave to cool.

(4) • Take the cakes out of the tin and spread the tops with the chocolate spread, using the butter knife.

• Break the crumbly chocolate bar into pieces and arrange on top of the cakes to look like nests. Add the mini eggs and chicks, if using.

Easter egg faces

Makes 1

ingredients

50 g (2 oz) dark chocolate

250 g (8 oz) white marzipan or ready-to-roll decoration icing

red, yellow and green paste food colourings

1 medium plain chocolate Easter egg

sifted icing sugar, for dusting

Cellophane and ribbon, for wrapping

equipment

small bowl

saucepan or microwave

small knife

chopping board

small rolling pin

small sieve

what to do

1 • Break the chocolate into pieces and melt in the bowl set over a saucepan of just boiled water. Alternatively, melt in the microwave for 1½ minutes on Full Power or according to manufacturer's instructions.

2 • Divide the marzipan or decoration icing into four pieces. Keep one piece white and colour the rest, using red, yellow and green food colourings.

3 • Unwrap the chocolate egg.

(4) • Roll out or mould small pieces of coloured marzipan or icing at a time into eyes, mouth, hair, ears, nose, feet and whatever features you would like your face to have. (Dust your hands and the work surface with a little sifted icing sugar if the marzipan or icing begins to stick.)

• Stick the facial features on to the eggs using dots of melted chocolate.

5 • Allow the decorated egg to harden. Wrap each egg in Cellophane and tie with ribbon.

Makes 4

equipment

chopping board

small serrated knife

teaspoon

ice cream scoop

halloween lanterns

ingredients

4 oranges

4 scoops vanilla ice cream or blackcurrant sorbet or set jelly

4 liquorice Catherine wheels

few glacé cherries

what to do

1. • On the chopping board, cut a slice off the top of each orange, about one-third down from the top, and put to one side.

   • Using the teaspoon, scoop out the orange flesh and membrane until you reach the white inside of the orange.

2. • Turn one of the oranges on its side and carefully cut eye and mouth shapes with the small sharp knife – get adult help if necessary. You may prefer to mark these on with a pen before you begin cutting. Do the same with the other oranges.

3. • Fill with scoops of ice cream, sorbet or jelly. Replace the lids, place sliced cherries into the mouths and add strips of unwound liquorice for hair. Serve immediately or put in the freezer until ready to serve.

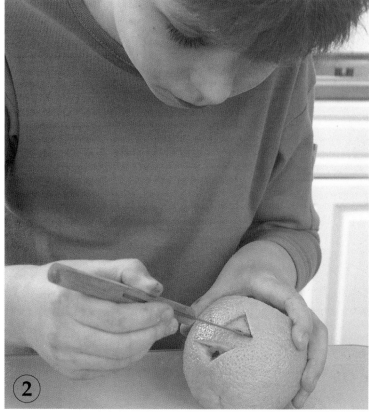

tips

★ Other fruits, such as a grapefruit, small watermelons or yellow-skinned melons, could also be used as lanterns.

★ Use the unused orange flesh to add to a fruit salad. Alternatively, to make a smoothie, blend the orange flesh with a banana and some yogurt in a liquidizer.

Makes 4

equipment

paper or thin piece of card

pen

kitchen scissors

chopping board

small knife

ghostly spooks

ingredients

4 slices bread

little butter or cream cheese, for spreading

4 slices of ham or cheese, the same size as the bread

4 pitted black olives

few slices carrot or red pepper

what to do

1 • Cut a square of paper or card the same size as the bread, then draw on a ghost shape and cut out.

② • On the chopping board, spread each slice of bread with butter or cream cheese and top with ham or cheese.

• Place the paper ghost shape over one open sandwich and cut around it with a small knife, with the bread still on the board. Repeat with other sandwiches.

3 • Halve the olives. Carefully cut zigzags in the carrot or red pepper slices for mouths.

• Decorate the ghosts with olives for eyes and jagged carrot or pepper mouths, all stuck in place with a little extra butter or cream cheese.

tip
★ Use this same idea to make other spooky
shapes for Halloween, perhaps a witch's
hat, cat or pumpkin lantern.

stained glass windows

Makes 12

equipment

2 baking sheets

nonstick baking paper

knife

chopping board or plate

mixing bowl

electric mixer (optional)

grater

rolling pin

selection of large and small biscuit cutters

ovengloves

ingredients

125 g (4 oz) butter

175 g (6 oz) plain flour

50 g (2 oz) caster sugar

½ small orange, rind only

few clear coloured boiled sweets

what to do

(1) • Set the oven to 180°C/350°F/Gas Mark 4.

• Line the baking sheets with the nonstick baking paper.

• Cut the butter into small squares, then put into the mixing bowl with the flour and sugar. Rub in the butter using your fingertips or an electric mixer until the mixture looks like fine crumbs (see page 15).

• Grate the orange rind finely, then stir it into bowl.

2 • Squeeze the mixture together with your hands to make a ball. Roll out thinly on a surface dusted with flour.

• Stamp out large window shapes using the biscuit cutters. Put on to the paper-lined sheets, then stamp out smaller shapes from the centre of each biscuit and remove.

tip

★ Similar biscuits can be made to hang on the Christmas tree, but use a firmer biscuit mixture, such as the one on page 138. Make tiny holes in the top of each biscuit with the end of a teaspoon as soon as they come out of the oven.

3 • Re-knead the biscuit trimmings, roll out and continue cutting biscuits until all the mixture is used.

• Bake in the oven for 8–10 minutes until pale golden.

4 • Meanwhile, unwrap the sweets and break with the rolling pin.

• Carefully remove the sheet of biscuits from the oven. Add different coloured pieces to the hole in each biscuit – get adult help with this because the biscuits will be hot.

• Bake in the oven for a further 2–3 minutes until the sweets have just melted.

• Leave to cool, then peel the biscuits off the paper and serve.

mini iced gingerbread

Makes 12

equipment

12 large muffin cases
12–hole deep muffin tin
saucepan
wooden spoon
sieve
2 bowls
jug
fork
ovengloves
spoon

ingredients

125 g (4 oz) butter

250 g (8 oz) golden syrup

75 g (3 oz) dark muscovado sugar

250 g (8 oz) self-raising flour

1 teaspoon ground ginger

1 teaspoon mixed spice

½ teaspoon bicarbonate of soda

150 ml (¼ pint) milk

2 eggs

125 g (4 oz) icing sugar

few sliced red, green and yellow glacé cherries or sweets

Cellophane and ribbon, to finish

what to do

1 • Set the oven to 180°C/350°F/Gas Mark 4.

• Place the muffin cases into the sections of the muffin tin.

2 • Put the butter, syrup and sugar into the saucepan. Heat the pan gently, stirring with the wooden spoon, until the butter has completely melted.

③ • Take the pan off the heat. Sift the flour, spices and bicarbonate into the bowl. Beat the milk and eggs together in the jug with the fork.

• Add the dry ingredients to the pan, mix with a wooden spoon, then gradually beat in the milk mixture until smooth.

③

④

4 • Half-fill the jug with the gingerbread mixture, then pour into the muffin cases until two-thirds full. Refill the jug and continue until all the cases are filled.

• Bake in the centre of the oven for 10–15 minutes until well risen and the tops spring back when pressed with the fingertips. Cool in the tin.

5 • Sift the icing sugar into the second bowl. Gradually mix in 4 teaspoons of water until a smooth thick icing.

• Arrange the cherries or sweets over the cakes and drizzle over the icing from the spoon in squiggly lines. Leave to set, then wrap individually in Cellophane and tie with ribbon.

chocolate tree decorations

Makes 22

equipment

2 baking sheets

pastry brush

saucepan

wooden spoon

sieve

bowl

rolling pin

large Christmas tree
  cutters or other festive
  cookie cutters

teaspoon

palette knife

ingredients

75 g (3 oz) butter

3 tablespoons golden
  syrup

150 g (5 oz) caster sugar

325 g (11 oz) plain flour

15 g (½ oz) cocoa

1 teaspoon ground
  cinnamon

2 teaspoons bicarbonate
  of soda

4 tablespoons milk

1 tube ready-to-use
white writing icing

mini candy-coated
  chocolate drops or
  other tiny sweets

fine ribbon, to finish

what to do

1 • Set the oven to 180°C/350°F/Gas Mark 4.

  • Brush the baking sheets with oil using the
    pastry brush.

  • Put the butter, syrup and sugar in the
    saucepan. Heat gently, stirring with a
    wooden spoon, until the butter has melted.

2 • Sift the flour, cocoa, cinnamon and
    bicarbonate of soda into the bowl, then
    add to the melted butter mixture with the
    milk. Mix to a smooth ball. Leave for 5
    minutes or until cool enough to handle.

3 • Knead until evenly coloured, then roll out on a lightly floured surface until it is 5 mm (¼ inch) thick.

• Stamp out Christmas shapes with the cutters, then transfer to the baking sheets. Re-roll the trimmings and continue cutting shapes until all the dough is used.

4 • Bake in the oven for 10–12 minutes until just beginning to darken. Make a hole in the top of each biscuit with the end of a teaspoon, then leave to cool on the sheets.

5 • Pipe on white icing to decorate by squeezing the icing straight from the tube. Decorate with sweets and leave to harden. Thread fine ribbon through the hole at the top of each biscuit, then tie on to the Christmas tree. Eat within 3 days.

tip

★ If the dough gets too stiff to re-roll the trimmings, warm the dough in the microwave on Full Power for 20–30 seconds, depending on the amount of dough.

Makes 25

equipment

mixing bowl or food
 processor

fork

sieve

wooden spoon

plastic gloves (optional)

trays

nonstick baking paper

boxes lined with waxed
 or greaseproof paper

candy canes

ingredients

1 sachet dried egg white
(or the equivalent of
2 egg whites)

few drops peppermint
essence

550 g (1 lb 2 oz) icing
sugar

little red liquid or paste
food colouring

what to do

1 • Put the dried egg white into the bowl or bowl of the food processor. Mix in the water with the fork – check with the packet instructions for the quantity.

• Add the peppermint essence, then gradually sift in the icing sugar, a little at a time, mixing with the wooden spoon to make a smooth paste. As the mixture gets stiffer, squeeze together with your hands.

2 • Add some red food colouring to the mixture and knead together, stopping when the colours are only half-mixed together and still look swirly. Use plastic gloves, if liked.

tip

★ For very young children, keep the mixture to just one colour, then roll out and stamp shapes using small biscuit cutters.

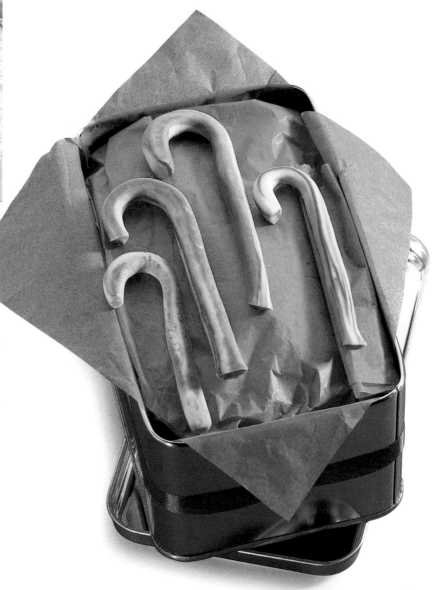

③ • Shape and roll pieces of icing into thin ropes on a work surface dusted with extra icing sugar until about 1 cm (½ inch) thick. Cut to 12 cm (5 inch) lengths. Curl the tops to resemble walking canes.

• Dry overnight on trays lined with nonstick baking paper.

4 • Pack the canes into small boxes lined with waxed or greaseproof paper. Use within 1 week.

index

Acknowledgements

The author and Publishers would like to thank Mex and Scarlet Adam; Kieran Aubrey; Chandani Amin; Lucy Broughton; Paula and Sophie Davies; Hamish and Sholto Douglas; Ella-Dee, Jessamy and Mayes Fusco; Dylan Gee; George Grylls; Natalie Harriet; Christian, Imogen and Mitch Hawksbee; Alice and William Lewis; Henrietta and Susanna Oram; and Archie Parker for being such wonderful models. They would also like to thank David and Daniella Cox for the kind loan of their home and Cadburys for providing chocolate eggs for the Festive Fun chapter.

Picture Acknowledgements

Octopus Publishing Group Limited/David Jordan 22 top left, 23, 24 left, 25, 26 left, 27, 28 left, 29, 30 left, 31, 32 left, 33 right, 34 left, 35, 36 left, 37, 38 left, 39 right, 40 top left, 41, 42 left, 43, 44 left, 45, 46 left, 47, 48 left, 49, 50 left, 51, 52 left, 53, 54 left, 55, 56 left, 57, 58 left, 59 bottom right, 60 left, 61, 62 left, 63 bottom, 64 left, 65, 66 left, 67, 68 top left, 69, 70 left, 71 right, 72 left, 73, 74 left, 75, 76 top left, 77, 78 top left, 79 right, 80 left, 81, 82 left, 83, 84 left, 85 right, 86 left, 87, 88 left, 89, 90 left, 91 bottom, 92 top left, 93 right, 94 left, 95, 96 left, 97, 98 left, 99, 100 left, 101, 102 left, 103 right, 104 left, 106 left, 107, 108 top left, 109, 110 left, 111, 112 left, 113, 114 left, 116 top left, 117, 118 left, 119, 120 left, 121, 122 left, 123, 124 left, 125 right, 126 top left, 127 bottom, 128 left, 129 right, 130 right, 130–131 bottom, 132 left, 133, 134 left, 135 right, 136 left, 137 right, 138 left, 139, 140 left, 141 right/Juliet Piddington 1 background, 3 background, 5 background, 6 background, 22 left, 40 left, 68 left, 78 left, 92 left, 108 left, 116 left, 126 left/Peter Pugh–Cook 1 centre left, 3, 6, 7, 8, 9, 10–11, 12–13, 14–15, 16–17, 18, 20–21, 22 right, 24 right, 26 right, 28 right, 30 right, 32 right, 33 left, 34 right, 36 right, 38 right, 39 left, 40 right, 42 right, 44 right, 46 right, 48 right, 50 right, 52 right, 54 right, 56 right, 58 right, 59 top left, 60 right, 62 right, 63 top, 64 right, 66 right, 68 right, 70 right, 71 left, 72 right, 74 right, 76 right, 78 right, 79 top left, 80 right, 82 right, 84 right, 85 left, 86 right, 88 right, 90 right, 91 top, 92 right, 93 left, 94 right, 96 right, 98 right, 100 right, 102 right, 103 left, 104 right, 106 right, 108 right, 110 right, 112 right, 114 right, 116 right, 118 right, 120 right, 122 right, 124 right, 125 left, 126 right, 127 top, 128 right, 129 left, 130 top right, 131 top, 132 right, 134 right, 135 left, 136 right, 137 left, 138 right, 140 right, 141 left

Executive Editor Nicola Hill
Managing Editor Clare Churly
Executive Art Editor Rozelle Bentheim
Designer Ruth Hope
Senior Production Controller Jo Sim
Food Stylist Sara Lewis
Special Photography David Jordan and Peter Pugh-Cook